How to Lead Smart People

Leadership for Professionals

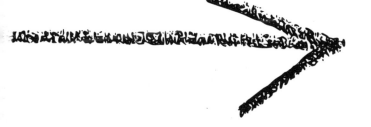

How to Lead Smart People

Leadership for Professionals

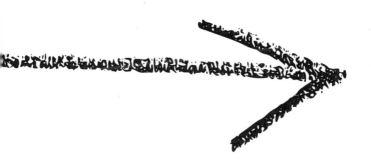

Arun Singh & Mike Mister

First published in Great Britain in 2019 by
Profile Books Ltd
3 Holford Yard
Bevin Way
London
WC1X 9HD
www.profilebooks.com

Printed and bound in Great Britain by Clays Ltd, Elcograf S.p.A.

The moral right of the authors has been asserted.

A complete catalogue record for this book can be obtained from the British Library on request.

ISBN 978 1 78816 154 1
eISBN 978 1 78283 494 6

For Syndi, Olivia and Stephanie (MM)

For my father Krishan, mother Chand,
wife Vineeta and daughters Amita and Asisa (AS)

Acknowledgements

We would like to thank our colleagues and friends at the Møller Institute, Alliance Manchester Business School, and the staff and facilities at the Law Society in Chancery Lane in London for providing us with a 'home from home' in which to write; Peter Jones and all at Profile Books for their serious levels of patience and ongoing support; our editor Clare Grist Taylor for making it readable; and Rob Lees, Iain MacLean and Rebecca Hill for undertaking considerable voluntary editorial support, providing helpful comments, precise criticism and helpful ideas.

We are indebted to the many thinkers and leaders with whom we have had the privilege to work over the years, including Professors Jack Gabarro, Ashish Nanda, Nitin Nohria, Das Narayandas, Narayan Pant, John Westwood, Adrian Furnham, Keith Murnighan, Paddy Miller, Steve Burnett, Elaine Ferneley, Gurnek Bains, Fons Trompenaars, Charles Hampden-Turner, and colleagues Des Woods, Liz Baltesz, Kevin Doolan, Susan David, Henry Marsden, Toby Hoskins, Morley Potter, David Jones, Andrew Hibbert, the late Tony Bunch, John Lucy, Andrew Wright and Tony Crossley. Whilst this list can never be complete we hope those who are not listed – you know who you are – will accept our sincere thanks.

Finally, and most importantly, we owe a huge debt of gratitude to the thousands of professionals and executives with whom we have had the privilege to work over the years. Their wisdom, wit, humour, friendship, encouragement and openness have been instrumental in informing our teaching and consulting.

Contents

Preface

Leading teams of knowledge workers and professionals presents an interesting challenge. People with these skills join organisations to do interesting, challenging work with equally smart, able people, applying their knowledge and experience for the benefit of their clients and their firms. They are smart people who, perhaps understandably, think they know everything already. They often don't believe they need leaders. They might not even believe in leadership itself. Unsurprisingly, leaders in the professions may have to work especially hard to earn the respect of the people they lead. Often this respect comes from being 'one of us', professionals themselves. So, what happens when professionals have to step up as leaders and learn a whole new, additional skill set on top of their technical skills and know-how? This is a book for these people – people like *you* – who also love the intellectual challenge and fun of the work, but are working hard to make sense of a leadership role they have been asked to perform, probably with little or no experience or training.

The material is based on hundreds of conversations with professionals and knowledge workers, from a range of industries and professions, all over the world. We have also included lots of practical advice from our many colleagues and the respected experts we work with, all of whom spend their time helping leaders to make sense of the challenges they face and to become better at what they do.

Each section is based on a topic we know has been an issue for the professionals we have worked with over the years. It is clearly a 'help' book, written for the express purpose of being 'dipped into' when you are in need of some ideas or guidance in a hurry. It is unashamedly not theoretical, nor is it intended to be read from start to finish; the How to use this book section (p. xii) outlines how the book is organised and can be used.

The advice is offered as practical steps based on hard-earned experience and counsel over the years. You should view the advice as something you would get from a trusted friend who's been there and done it before. Frankly, this is the sort of material and ideas we wish we had been given earlier in our careers. We hope it helps.

Arun Singh and Mike Mister

How to use this book

How to Lead Smart People offers advice and guidance on some of the key topics and issues you're likely to face as a leader of smart people, organised into three parts:

Part 1: Leading Me
Focuses on your own performance as a manager.

Part 2: Leading the Team
Shows you how to work with different people and achieve a high-performing team.

Part 3: Leading the Organisation
Teaches you how to build your profile outside of your team.

Each topic has its own section, and each section follows the same format:

An **Introduction** explains the topic or issue that will be covered, followed by an **Example** based on our experience. Then we have an action-oriented **Do this** section, consisting of **Try this/Like this** grids which, rather than offering high-level solutions, try to be very clear and specific about what you might try to do in a given situation. At the end of each section, we sum up with a few snappy closing thoughts: **And remember**.

Bear in mind that the advice is offered without the benefit of knowing your specific context. It should therefore be treated as all good, well-meaning advice should be treated: considered against the situation with which you are dealing. If it suggests a course of action or ideas that will help address your issue, then put it into your own words and see how it works for you.

To get you started, here's an example of the Do this section:

Do this

→ **Dip in and dip out**
Pick the topic that you need help with or have interest in. If it does not appear in the Index, look for other topics that might be connected and try them. The overview of each topic outlines what is being covered and why we consider it important.

→ **Check out the ideas that we suggest**
Ask yourself: how would that work in my circumstance, in the situation with which I am faced? Consider the ideas and suggestions and tailor them to your issue and your organisation. And be sure to use trusted colleagues and confidant(e)s to check out what you are proposing. Their advice will give you another perspective.

→ **Keep things moving**
Take action; make things happen. Inaction breeds fear, concern, worry and uncertainty. Leadership is about acting, movement, going forward.

→ Rehearse with a friend

Grab a friend and actually practise/rehearse the conversations you need to have. This is not the same as checking out your ideas as noted above. We mean actually practise the conversation with your friend. Say the actual words you intend to use and ask how they were received. Did they have the impact and desired result? What might need to be changed?

→ Use this book as a starting point

Make time to read more widely about leadership and management, but beware of the latest trend or fad that is hitting the bookshelves. This book is written for busy, smart people looking for ideas and help when they are in a hurry. It is no substitute for a more detailed study of the subjects of leadership and management.

And remember

In our work with hundreds of professionals we are regularly asked 'How do I . . .?', 'What would you do . . .?', or even the ubiquitous 'I have a friend who . . .' . Our experience tells us that busy people are looking for quick, practical and effective tips that will help them make a difference as leaders. In this book we have tried to offer just that: the advice that you would get from a trusted friend or colleague who has been there and done it before; the sort of quiet conversation you would have over coffee or a drink. Dip in, experiment and use the book when you need a quick solution to a problem you're facing right now, when time is tight and you need to act.

Leading smart people

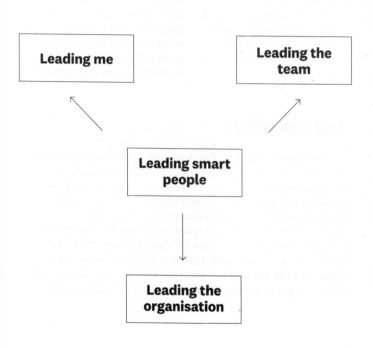

1.
Leading Me

Assertiveness

Assertiveness can be a tricky skill to develop. It benefits hugely from focused practice. There is a thin line between assertiveness and aggression and it is easy, even for smart people, to mix them up. So what's the difference? Assertiveness is related to balance, being clear about your needs and taking into consideration the needs of others. Aggression is based on winning without any thought of the rights or feelings of others and might even be seen as bullying.

Assertiveness, your assertiveness, is entwined with the idea of 'rights and values' and judgement, those 'rights' you think you have and those you afford or deny others. Smart leaders don't dominate non-assertive people but include and involve them. Equally, smart people resist the pressure of excessively dominant or aggressive behaviour. Being assertive protects one from being taken advantage of, and helps to achieve one's own goals and reduce anxiety. It also protects those less capable of exercising or expressing their own rights.

Assertiveness is about making choices and should be used selectively as part of your overall range of behaviours, dialled up or down depending on the situation or context.

Example

Angela was on a call when Mark, the partner to whom she reported, entered her office without knocking. Mark stood in front of her, his impatience palpable as he waited for the call to finish. As soon as she put the phone down, Mark leapt in: 'I need you to prepare a talk for me to give to an international conference in Rome next week.' Angela, a senior associate, was speaking at the same conference and had already completed 60 per cent of her preparation. Angela always found it difficult to say 'No' and usually worked whatever hours it took to get a job done, something Mark was well aware of and had exploited in the past.

Angela was also aware that she was being considered for promotion and had a pile of other work to complete before the conference. She thought to herself, 'Do I really have to do this or am I just pleasing someone else?' She realised she had the right to say 'No' in an assertive, adult manner. Her 'mind talk' – what she was saying to herself – was clear: 'No, I do not have to do this now.' In response to escalating pressure from Mark, she replied: 'I appreciate you need to get this done, Mark, but I am unable to deliver what you need in the time available.' As Mark continued to press her, Angela, secure in her thinking about her rights, made steady eye contact and with firm, open hand gestures confirmed, 'I know you need help, Mark, but it is just not possible for me to deliver for you just now.'

Mark left her office to find someone else to prepare the paper for him. Angela felt surprisingly calm and justified in the way she had judged the situation, stood her ground and quietly, yet assertively, refused the request.

Do this

→ **Be aware of your rights and value them**

Having self-belief and clearly knowing your goals builds self-confidence to assert your rights and needs with clarity. To perform to your full potential, you need to ensure that your needs are clearly articulated. Write down the rights to which you think you are realistically entitled: to make requests, to ask, to say 'No', to query deadlines.

→ **Try 'fogging' responses**

The idea of 'fogging' means listening carefully to what is being said, acknowledging the elements that are true, but not getting drawn into or feeling pressured to agree to either explicit or implicit demands from the other person. It is especially helpful if someone is placing pressure on you, but you do not want to carry out the task because it is not in your best interests. Listen to the person. Reply using their vocabulary, acknowledge their need, but state your view. This way you are showing them that you have understood their request but you cannot adhere to it. For example, a response to a request that 'I need this now!' might, using the 'fogging' technique, be: 'I am sure you do, but it is just not possible now, as my priority is ...'

→ **Accept that you cannot control the behaviours of others**

If colleagues react to your assertiveness in an angry or resentful way, do not react to them in the same way. You can only control your own behaviour, so stay calm and measured to help dissipate the anger. Be respectful and say or remake your request assertively.

→ **Learn and practise saying 'No'**

When you do have to say 'No', try to explore an alternative solution that works for everyone. This can be hard, but it's critical if you want to become more assertive. For example, understand how much work you are able to take on and identify any areas of your work where you feel you are being taken advantage of, but also come up with some ideas for how that work might be reallocated. Or suggest how the work can be rescheduled to accommodate the request over the longer term.

→ Try 'scripting'

Pretend you are writing dialogue for a play and write down your opening form of words and how you want to deliver them assertively, outlining four steps: the situation, your feelings, your needs and the consequences. Keep it brief and succinct. Then practise saying the sentence(s) out loud, paying attention to the delivery. Scripting is really useful if you find it difficult to express your feelings clearly and confidently. One proviso: do not try and script the entire conversation, as you never know exactly how the other person will respond.

→ Change your verbs

Use more definite and emphatic verbs to give a clear message. Use 'I want', 'I need' or 'I feel' to express basic assertions. Use verbs like 'will' instead of 'could' or 'should', 'want' instead of 'need', and 'choose to' instead of 'have to'. For example: 'I choose this alternative option because I think it will be more successful than the other options before us.'

→ Try being a scratched record – use repetition

Prepare the message that you want to convey ahead of time. If the person does not get the message, then keep repeating your message using the same words; be relentless.

→ Think about your responsibilities

While you have the right to make requests yourself, you also have the responsibility to listen to the other person's response and treat it sensitively. Ignoring or just brushing aside their point of view is aggressive or bullying behaviour. Taking a weak or poor refusal at face value may be seen as unassertive, but rights and responsibilities must be balanced.

And remember

Being assertive is about finding the right balance between passivity and aggression and being firm about what you want and why. It helps to have a firm and clear sense of yourself and the goals you want to achieve, a self-belief that you deserve to get what you want and to stand up for yourself, even in challenging situations. Smart people express their needs and wants in a positive way. They know when and how to say 'no' firmly and use assertive communication techniques to communicate their thoughts and feelings firmly and directly, enhanced by appropriate body language (see the section on Body language, p. 17). It takes practice to become assertive. Smart people find mastering assertiveness helps them to become more productive, to have more power and control over themselves, and to earn the respect of their colleagues.

Authenticity

Being authentic is about having a strong sense of inner character: being true to yourself. It is about integrity in all your dealings and interactions. As with assertiveness, this means recognising your central values, inner worth, and what you are happy and not happy to do. To be authentic you have to know who and what you are, which you gain through self-reflection and feedback. It requires courage to stand back from the crowd, but it is a critical component of trust and an intrinsic part of the bond between leaders and followers. People will trust you if you keep your word and if you are consistent. Predictable behaviour also builds a climate of psychological safety. Your colleagues want to know that you stand for things that they feel are important and that you are prepared to support them actively.

Example

Carlos was on a guaranteed track for equity partnership in his firm. He had joined after qualification and had become well regarded by both his peers and team members. It was fully expected that he would be admitted to the partnership. He knew from conversations initiated by senior partners that he was to be proposed for partnership in the coming promotion cycle. However, he had doubts as to whether he was ready to step up. He knew it would require intense and frequent travel over the next 12 to 18 months and was concerned about the impact on his preschool children. He also knew that he would have to get up to speed in a new area of work in order to be able to advise his clients. He decided that he needed to delay things and initiated a conversation with his departmental head to stay the process for 12 months. His boss was very understanding and Carlos was assured he would be given due consideration in the next promotion round.

He then had to decide how best to communicate this difficult decision to his team and peers. The easy way out would be to say that he had not been chosen this year. Instead, Carlos told his immediate peers exactly what he had done and why. He then thought carefully about how best to handle the inevitable questions from his team, all the while being honest and taking full responsibility for his decision. He was made a partner the following year and eventually became one of the most respected leaders in the firm, known for his straight talking and his empathy, recognised as a 'go-to person' for sound, pragmatic advice.

Do this

→ **Have a personal manifesto**
Set a personal vision; decide what is important to you and what you are trying to achieve. Share this vision about yourself – in appropriate measure – with your people. Who are you? What do you stand for? What is it like working with you? What gets you mad? Happy? Upset? Proud?

→ **Allow people in**
Share with your people the 'why' behind your thinking and decisions – and make it personal: tell formative stories and experiences from your career so that people can understand the 'why' you've chosen.

→ **Be consistent**
Make your actions reflect your words and make sure your words really mean the things you intend to do. Do not say things you do not mean. Consistently acting with integrity, in both your work and personal life, demonstrates a strong sense of character.

→ **Establish boundaries**
Make your boundaries semi-permeable. As people show interest, share more information but don't go too far too fast. The more people know you, the more they will understand you and what drives and is important to you. But set this pace carefully; being too open with everyone from the get-go is potentially as damaging, and off-putting, as being completely closed to them.

→ **Know when to stop**
Be clear on what you won't share. Your people need to understand there will be occasions when you are constrained by cabinet responsibility, but you will tell them everything you can as soon as you can.

There will be times when you prefer not to be so open, but think about how this will be perceived. If it might impact negatively on others' perceptions of your trustworthiness and the image they hold of you, reconsider your position.

→ **Be transparent**
Open communication is part of the DNA of authenticity. Understanding, recognising

and appreciating your flaws will make you more self-confident and secure. So share stories (see the section on Storytelling, p. 221) of when you have failed or things have not worked out as you planned and what you learnt from it. You will exude a presence of being self-confident and grounded.

People, particularly those who may not be grounded or are lacking in self-confidence, are drawn to those they feel they can trust.

→ **Have a range of styles – but constant values**

Use different styles with your team depending on the individuals you are working with. But stay constant in your values. Smart people have an inbuilt detector for inconsistencies.

And remember

We all have multiple dimensions of ourselves that we present to different groups in the outside world. The key to authenticity is letting your people get close enough so they understand what you stand for: your values; your priorities; how you will respond under different circumstances. It's about sharing enough of you so that others will make the decision to trust and follow you.

Authenticity doesn't mean sharing every facet of your life with your colleagues. They are, after all, your colleagues not your life partner. But it does mean being open with them, sharing hopes, fears, concerns, aspirations and worries. And doing so in a way that does not make them unduly fearful, but leaves them feeling positive, uplifted and enabled to deal with the future.

Consistency is the key. Saying and doing need to go hand in hand, so that what your colleagues see is what they get.

Being an energy radiator

As a leader, job number 1 is to keep your followers enthused and aligned to your purpose: you are seeking that discretionary extra effort that only comes from engagement. Nobody wants to work in an environment that is miserable and downbeat; such environments often spiral downwards and the reputation of the leader with them. You need to pay close attention to the messages that you give to help your people feel good about themselves and what they are doing. Giving praise, acknowledging people and their efforts, and providing clarity about how their work contributes to a bigger, better, more positive future are key. One proviso: smart people know when they have done good work, but they also know when they have not. Balancing your radiating energy with the need to recognise effort judicially is a critical skill. Above all, being honest with your team is essential.

Example

Ricardo was managing partner for about a thousand highly qualified people in four different geographical locations. His people seemed to all love and/or respect him. It was almost impossible to find someone with a bad word to say about him. How had he achieved this near miracle?

Ricardo was recognised for his plain speaking and made a point of connecting with people at every opportunity. He made time for everyone from his peers to the most junior person in the business. When something had to be said it was delivered with candour, respect and sensitivity. But it was always delivered. He visited his offices regularly, circulating his leadership team meetings between locations so that the leadership team could mix with every member of staff.

One visit to a large office, spread over several floors, was typical. He took the elevator to the top floor of the building and made his way down, stopping on every floor and chatting with people as he wandered past their desks, sometimes about work, sometimes about their personal life. His conversations were always upbeat, focusing on opportunities, finding solutions to problems, connecting people, or offering praise or feedback.

Each visit ended with a dinner with a different group of invited staff: new hires on one, newly promoted staff on another, administrative and functional staff on another. While it took time, it also resulted in some of the highest staff engagement scores – and per capita profitability – in the entire organisation. The energy and positivity Ricardo radiated were infectious.

Do this

→ **Be visible**
Lead by walking about and connecting with your people. But take care not to be seen to favour any one person or group more than any other. Try to build a cohesive group and keep as many people engaged as possible. Smart people are invariably creative.

→ **Use technology**
Use technology to connect and catch up with your people if your group is too widely dispersed to meet physically.

→ **Connect with as many people as possible**
Use every opportunity to speak directly with your people. Listen to them and show that you have listened by repeating their issues back to them and asking what help they need to get them resolved. Add in your ideas, and ensure you follow up with any offers of help or assistance you have made.

→ **Explain your decisions**
Have clear decision-making criteria that you are prepared to share, especially for contentious decisions. This will help others to understand why decisions have been made. Smart people are often creative and if you don't explain your decisions they will make up their own reasons for your actions – which may not be as positive as your intent.

→ **Encourage your people**
Smart people want to be the best they can be, so find ways to help them get better. It may simply be encouragement, or recognising them and their efforts. You might help them to solve a problem or connect them with others who might help. The crucial thing is that you have noticed them and shown interest in them as people.

→ **Project positivity**
Find ways of seeing the positive, even in the most trying circumstances. But make sure you are being realistic. Smart people see through unfounded optimism. Be upbeat and positive without appearing naïve or simplistic. Recognise concerns, treat them seriously, and help your people find ways forward.

→ Watch your language

Start saying 'Yes and' instead of 'Yes but'. 'And' builds connections. Smart people will pick up on small slips of language so make sure you phrase things in a positive and forward-looking manner.

→ Celebrate effort as well as success

Recognise effort as well as success. In the main, smart people come to work to do a good job. They pride themselves on doing good work and are often overly self-critical if things have not worked out as planned. So make sure that you recognise their efforts as well as their successes. Recognising effort as a contribution to knowledge in the department is a good way of making sure you are not rewarding failure for its own sake.

→ Be approachable

Encourage your people to speak with you about anything. Initiate conversations and stay relentlessly curious about how your people are faring. Some people may feel that they should keep things from you or that you are too important or busy to be bothered with them and their concerns. Make it clear that you expect to be approached. This may need to be managed, but the principle of open access should be paramount.

→ Keep perspective

Help people to see beyond difficulties or crises. When things have not gone well, encourage a sense of perspective. Time pressures and urgency may make things seem far worse than they really are. Smart leaders and smart people who are focused on their own work can easily lose sight of the bigger picture. For them it may appear to be a huge problem or issue but the reality may be substantively different.

And remember

Being an energy radiator can be an energy-draining experience for you personally. Inevitably there will be times when circumstances 'get' to you and you might need to remind your people that you're human too. But it's important not to let this last too long. Having strategies to recharge and replenish yourself are vitally important. Think about who *your* energy radiator is. Where do you go to get an energy fix to enable you to start afresh, to keep energised and enthused? It may be an individual or group of friends or family; it might be a routine you have established for yourself, a place to go or an activity you love. Whatever it is, make sure you are looking after yourself. That includes your personal regime, taking vacations, getting rest and downtime. Self-care will help you keep up the energy levels you need and is crucial for effective leadership.

Body language

Body language is the silent language that smart leaders use to both interpret and convey reactions, feelings and attitudes. They do this through observing and using body movements, facial expressions, tone and loudness of voice, hand gestures, postures, handshakes. To an accomplished practitioner, all the little and not so little things we register when we are in someone's presence are like listening to a silent orchestra.

For many professionals their training has taught them to be 'low reactors' in terms of their behaviour, and it can be difficult to gauge levels of enthusiasm or resistance for ideas and proposals.

Understanding body language is therefore a really helpful tool when leading smart people. Leaders who practise until they can intuitively read the body language of others find it helps them communicate more effectively and empathically. They are also able to manage their own body language consciously to bring emphasis, authority and power to their messages.

Example

Kiran let out a resigned sigh. She had just received an email from Don, the CEO of the start-up on the tech park where she was the lead researcher. It was bad news; her research proposal had not been approved by investors.

It seemed very odd. She had met with Don and he had been very positive about the proposal. Her presentation had been detailed, maybe a trifle long, and she recalled Don had repeatedly checked the time on his watch. He had made minimal eye contact, and kept looking out of the window. Kiran assumed he was thinking about the forthcoming shareholders' call. He mumbled, 'Great idea, Kiran. It has legs and the kind of original ideas that the investors like.'

If Kiran had known a little bit more about body language, she would also have noticed him doodling on his pad, sitting on the edge of his chair as if he was about to leave, and that he was tapping his fingers 10 minutes into her presentation.

On reflection she realised she should have been paying more attention to Don's behaviour. With hindsight it had spoken volumes, indicating his impatience and signalling her to finish. For the future she realised she needed to pay much closer critical attention to the body language of her audience. If she had, she would have understood better that her presentation was not doing justice to her proposal, she could have discussed its shortcomings with Don, and there would have been a much higher chance of it being accepted by the investors. And as Kiran's CEO, Don should also have been more aware of his own body language and listened to what it was telling him: that the proposal was not ready, and that he needed to have an open conversation with Kiran about how it might be improved.

Do this

→ **Observe hands**

Be aware of what your hands are doing and the messages they might be sending. People who keep their hands visible are usually viewed as more transparent. A firm handshake with the meeting of the palms (but not too firm or too long) can convey calm assertiveness and confidence in front of others. Someone who is stressed or nervous may display quivering hands or a limp handshake, neither of which are likely to instil confidence.

→ **Eye contact**

Hold the other person's gaze and look at the person when you are speaking together. This implies sincerity, interest and engagement with the subject matter. But avoid a staring match as this can be construed as confrontational.

→ **Sit comfortably still in meetings**

Sit still and calmly without fidgeting. Focus your attention on making eye contact and watching the behaviour of your colleagues while you listen to them. It indicates that you are interested in what is being said, grounded and self-assured.

→ **Adopt an open posture**

An open posture means directly facing someone, hands apart, communicating openness or interest in someone and a readiness to listen. A closed posture with arms folded, legs crossed or positioned at a slight angle from the person with whom they are interacting can indicate discomfort or lack of interest.

→ **Remember that body language is cultural**

Check out where you are and who you are with. For example, in Western culture it is perfectly acceptable (and encouraged) to debate issues with everyone in the group. In some Asian cultures there is still a deference shown for age; directly contradicting an elder is seen as the height of discourtesy and rudeness. A little research can save a lot of embarrassment and misunderstanding.

→ **Don't jump to conclusions**

When interpreting others' body language, verify your initial instincts. Yes, a person with folded arms, a tense facial expression or not making eye contact is exhibiting stereotypical negative indicators. But they may have a good reason, such as a bad headache or a preoccupation with something else that is going on in their life. Use questions and conversation to find out.

→ **Check your assumptions**
Test in your own mind why you are interpreting behaviour in a given way. That person who is talking to their colleague whilst you are presenting: are they just talking or does one of them have poor language skills and is their colleague translating or explaining for them? Similarly, when other people are using technology, are they really catching up on email or simply using their device to make notes?

And remember

Body language is a really important part of how we communicate; just look at how much we can lose when communicating by only phone, text or email. The expression 'looking people in the eye' when giving certain messages is also telling. It is as though we gain something extra from the proximity – and we do: the many, many micro-signals we detect from watching another's face. Paying attention to behaviour by close observation, and becoming proficient in detecting these signals, provides valuable clues about feelings and emotions. It can help us understand the complete message of what someone is trying to say to us. While it is clearly dangerous to make universal assumptions based on a single observation, with practice, and over time, a smart person can develop the skill of interpreting body language to gain insight into the real message being given or how it is truly being received.

The important leadership message is to look for patterns of behaviour, especially when we feel we are getting mixed signals; are the words and behaviour consistent? If your conversation partner crosses their arm in front of you, are they being defensive? Are they cold? Or just getting comfortable? That's the time to check your interpretation through questioning and further conversation. Understanding body language is an important part of the toolkit leaders need to be effective communicators.

Building trust

Smart leaders know that trust is absolutely fundamental to their leadership. Your people have to trust you – and you have to trust them. It is the lubrication that makes relationships and organisations work and helps create a willingness for others to take action in situations where they may feel vulnerable or unsure or where the situation is ambiguous.

However, trust is also fragile and easily undermined by a misplaced word, phrase or action. It is a product of expressed intention: how you think about what you might do, the behaviours you exhibit to turn intention into action, and how that is experienced by the other party. It is built up over time on a basis of repeated interactions. Those repeated interactions enable the other person to gauge your reactions in any given circumstance. This is important because it provides a degree of psychological safety for team members.

Consistency in intent and behaviour is essential when leading, and probably even more important when leading smart people, who see any inconsistencies quickly and in very sharp relief.

Example

David was sending an associate, Asisa, abroad for a sensitive matter for a key client. He had thought long and hard about who to send, carefully reviewing the bright young high-flyers in his group before deciding to send her.

In truth Asisa had not immediately stood out from her peer group. However, over the 18 months of working with David, she had become much more visible. She always delivered her work on time or slightly early and was proactive in raising queries and issues with him. When he tested her with more complex issues, she had demonstrated that she had done the research and sought advice from other, more senior colleagues. She regularly drafted communications for him that needed very little amendment. In client interactions he increasingly let her take a bigger role and was pleased to see the way her style was showing a degree of maturity in the way she questioned and dealt with the clients.

On Asisa's return to the office, David was gratified to hear from the client that they were very impressed with the maturity and tact with which Asisa had handled the assignment. He realised that the decision to send her was more than justified by the feedback from a very grateful client. The trust that had built up between them over repeated positive interactions had led to a good outcome for both of them.

Do this

→ **Keep your promises**
Keep your word and commitments. If you promise to read a draft, make an introduction, speak to an influencer on someone's behalf, look into a career development course for someone, then do it. Ask your team for feedback on how you are doing, and act on it.

→ **Get to know colleagues personally**
There is no substitute for face-to-face interaction. Smart leaders use tools such as Monday morning meetings which are standing only (no chairs allowed!), in which the team can talk about what they did over the weekend and share their interests, before getting to the business agenda for the meeting. They also regularly share work problems and ideas. This uses the whole team's experience to develop competence and trust. Not all of this is strictly business, but it helps with familiarity, and familiarity breeds trust. Investing time and effort to help people to get to know each other on a personal and human level helps to create the ties that bind.

→ **Be transparent**
Transparency is important during both good and tough times. Share what you are feeling good about, but also issues and causes for concern. Explain the basis for decisions and show candour about problems. Your people need to know and understand the 'big picture'.

→ **Express your feelings**
Smart leaders who can convey their feelings along with hard facts are seen as more approachable and therefore more trustworthy.

→ **Share your knowledge about your product, service and sector**
Discuss new technical and sector trends with colleagues. It is no use being a leader with technical knowledge that your team cannot access. Being generous with your knowledge and approachable for guidance will encourage your team to seek you out. They are also more likely to understand and accept your direction and decisions.

→ Trust your team

Invite team members to lead presentations and projects and encourage them to take and run with new initiatives. Trust is reciprocal. Displaying trust in the team's knowledge, skills and decision-making instils in them a trust of the smart leader.

→ Be fair

Be objective and impartial when giving reviews and rewards. Take the blame if it's due to you, and give and share credit where it is due.

→ Keep confidences

Keep confidences; this is fundamental to trustworthiness. Followers require discretion and reliance, a genuine belief and feeling that a leader will not betray their confidence.

→ Be consistent

Smart leaders know that their people seek predictability. Trust relies upon expectation and consistent actions.

And remember

Leadership cannot be effective without trust. You need to understand how to earn that trust, and how you build trust in others. It is about consistency in your intentions, your words and your actions. It is about building straight-talking relationships so that both sides have a track record of experience that enables each to predict the other's reactions in any given set of circumstances. It is about being clear about your motives, saying what you propose to do – and then doing it, time after time after time.

Leading smart people means helping them become the best they can be for the organisation and themselves. That means they need to be able to stretch themselves and venture into places that, for them, may be 'risky'. To do that, they need the security of being able to trust their leaders. Being trustworthy makes you the leader with whom others will want to work; smart people will only follow leaders they trust.

Developing you for the future

We often meet leaders who are so time-poor that they neglect themselves. As a leader of smart people this is a dangerous place to be. Smart people recognise and know when others are as smart or informed as them. They know when others can do things better than them and are able to identify people with insight that can make a difference. Smart people also recognise different sorts of capabilities: even if you are not the smartest professional in your group, they will recognise that you might have different competencies, such as practice management skills, industry knowledge or client-handling expertise.

Information today has little value. It is almost freely available via the Internet and in abundance. That we now have a phrase to describe this function – Google it – is a testament to just how much 'stuff' is out there and accessible. The important thing is no longer just what you know or where to go to find out. It's about how you turn what you know, or what you can find out, into insight that is useful and therefore valuable to you in future.

Example

Ahmed was a tax specialist, and absolutely thrilled when he got the call to join a government task force advising on the introduction of goods and services taxes. Although never an outstanding fee earner, his practice had provided a regular source of income for the firm, maintaining a small team that serviced a local client base.

His new role on the task force gave him the opportunity to develop himself, despite the fact that these new programmes and responsibilities were outside his comfort zone. Although he had a heavy client workload, he delegated work to free up time to attend classes. At his annual appraisal his boss advised him to do even more, and he began to teach others on the firm's knowledge management programmes and support product development.

Over a short period of time Ahmed had moved from being a relatively unknown client servicer into an important contributor to the firm's intellectual capital, innovative service offerings, better business developers and client-service team leaders. He was fast-tracked to partnership. Taking the time to invest in his own personal development and understanding how he could make a real difference transformed both his career prospects and his contribution to his firm.

Do this

→ **Make a plan for you**
Figure out what you need to know or be able to do to make yourself more valuable in the future. Identify short-term (six-month) and medium-term (two-year) goals linked to, and part of, your personal agenda. When you have figured that out, work out how to acquire the knowledge, skill or experience you'll need. Be creative. Ask for help from your mentors or HR teams. A training course is *unlikely* to be the very best way.

→ **Be ready for your next role**
Think about where you want your career to go next. Identify the next step you wish to take and build a plan to get yourself there. This should be part of your agenda.

→ **Find a mentor**
Find someone who can challenge your ideas, pass on wisdom and help guide your thinking. This may not always be an older person: for trends, ideas and new thinking, a younger mentor (reverse mentoring) could be better. (See the section on Mentoring, p. 200.)

→ **Listen to career experts**
In most cities, many consulting firms offer free 'taster' sessions, usually over breakfast. Get on mailing lists. Listen to the speakers, and find opportunities to apply what you have learnt. If you need help, ask your HR or learning and development people to help you find entry points. You may even make some new contacts.

→ **Reconnect with your university or business school**
Most universities or business schools welcome their alumni. Many run short taster sessions, usually in the evenings. Make a point of attending regularly to help build your network and give you access to other networks. It's a great place to keep connected and meet other alumni who may be of help in the future.

→ **Do different stuff**
Find somewhere to go or something to do for a day every three or four months that is outside your comfort zone. Teach, visit a client's factory, get a role as a fundraiser or on a charity board. Shadow an

executive in another business. Just do something different. Comfort zones are bad.

→ Conferences are good

Attend, but with clear aims in mind, such as hearing certain speakers or meeting new people. Take a colleague to compare notes or go to separate sessions for two lots of input. Most importantly, share what you've learnt with your team when you get back.

→ Reading is good, so is your computer

Reading books in whatever form is good, but don't ignore things like TED (Technology, Entertainment, Design) talks or other management and leadership content on the Web. You'll find there a wealth of information that you can turn into insight. Think about what will help your colleagues and clients. One proviso: beware unsubstantiated content that has little or no empirical basis.

→ Go where your clients go

Find out what your clients or customers do to support personal development, especially open or public programmes. Then go along, or ask if you can attend one of their in-house sessions, either as a participant or a contributor. This is all about increasing your credibility and visibility. But always remember that you also need to be one step ahead of your clients; it's good to go where your clients go, but also seek stretching opportunities to go beyond current thinking and practice.

→ Make reflection a routine

Find the time and space for reflection. Diarise a regular slot every week, noting something that you have learnt. Keep a record so that you have up-to-date examples and experience that can be shared with those who have influence over your career.

→ Be ready for the next role

Update your CV/résumé every three to six months. Include what you have done, learnt and experienced over the last three months. This helps to build capability, as well as resilience and confidence in one's own capabilities. Diarise it and do it.

And remember

Most executives and professionals struggle to find more than a few hours each year for their own growth and development, in spite of the fact that most professional institutes and bodies have a requirement for some sort of CPE/D (Continuing Professional Education/Development). Would you entrust your health to a professional who spent so little time and effort in keeping up to date? Your doctor or dentist, perhaps? No, probably not.

Think about using some of the time you have allocated to CPE/D to do something other than technical updates. As a minimum, every year book yourself a few days to go away and do something educational rather than work-related. Go on a factory visit, go to a conference, visit your local business school. Offer to go and teach something somewhere to someone. *Do something different*. Whatever you do, the important thing is to keep investing in yourself; it's the only way to future-proof your career and your business.

Emotional intelligence

Leaders of smart people know that their people are more willing to deliver and push themselves for someone they like, respect and trust. And the judgements they make about their leader's likeability, and ability to command respect and trust, are heavily based on the behaviour that they experience. Often these judgements are made without too much conscious thought. Human behaviour is driven, in the main, by emotions.

Leaders who are in touch with their emotions know how they feel themselves, and are able to read and understand how others feel. In reality we can never really know how another feels; our lived experience is different to theirs (one reason why the expression 'I know how you feel' is so grating, especially to smart people). But we can empathise and we can try to manage our own behaviour in such a way that it encourages positive responses from others. Leaders of smart people have a good understanding of how their emotions are seen and might be experienced by others. They use this insight to uplift and empower their colleagues.

Example

Out of the blue Mary was told she was to be considered for partnership in a big international corporate advisory firm. The detailed process of assessment and interviews was about to be triggered. Instead of being excited, Mary became panicked and stressed. Her mind was cluttered with 'Is this my last chance?', 'Am I up to it?', 'I have so much work on my plate and business I have no space to focus and prepare'.

The partner who was proposing Mary's candidature recognised that she was fast becoming her own worst enemy. He set up a meeting for her with Geoff, who was responsible for developing the firm's senior talent.

As Mary walked in to his office, Geoff immediately observed that her energy level was low. Her shoulders were drooping, her body movements were jerky, and her speech was very fast. Geoff recognised her state and immediately offered her some water. He sat her down and said, 'Mary, the first thing that we need to agree is that we are going to have a good outcome from this meeting.' By that one comment he relaxed her, created a safe environment, and centred her emotions. He got her attention and they started to work out how she should approach the partnership admission process. Later, in conversation with her own associates, Mary often cited that conversation as pivotal in shifting her attitude towards the assessment process and helping her pass with flying colours. By being able to identify and empathise with how Mary was feeling, and offering some strategies for managing these emotions, Geoff taught her a valuable lesson she was able to draw on in future, both for herself and with other colleagues.

Do this

→ **Identify and name your emotional reaction**
Pay attention to what is happening to you physically. Know what causes you stress. How does it feel when you start to panic? Know your 'hot' buttons and manage them. Understand your emotions and control your feelings; don't let them rule you. And learn to trust your intuition.

→ **Recognise your emotions are just signals**
Check your current reality and decide if your emotional signals are misplaced. Listen to how your emotions are affecting you. The signals your emotions are sending you are probably based on echoes and memories from the past. Now be realistic: is that the reality of this current situation? It may not be. Almost certainly the circumstances now are different.

→ **Self-regulate**
Practise being calm; focus and breathe deeply. Smart people tend not to make rushed emotional decisions or stereotype people. They exercise a degree of self-control. Take time and pace yourself. Leaders who regulate themselves can better control their emotions and resist impulsive behaviours.

→ **Learn to be empathic**
Identify with and understand the wants, needs and viewpoints of your colleagues. Recognising the feelings of others enhances your relationships and your ability to listen, helping you avoid prejudicial decisions.

→ **Take a perceptual position**
Stand in other people's shoes. Why do they perceive the world differently to you? What is their perspective of a situation? When you can imagine how others feel, you understand them better and can lead more effectively.

→ **Take responsibility for your actions**
If you hurt a colleague's feelings, apologise. Don't ignore your action; it will fester and the other person may avoid you. Saying you are sorry is powerful. Smart people are much more respectful and willing to forgive if you acknowledge and correct mistakes or negative behaviours.

→ Recognise the signs

Learn to observe behaviour in others. Watch out for small, unusual behaviours that are out of the norm, words and phrases that give clues to what others are feeling. Act upon those clues. Do people need more or less time with you? Is there something they are trying to tell you? Be particularly vigilant when the pressure is on: our emotional reactions often override our good intentions at times of stress.

→ Self-development

Consider whether you need to improve your self-awareness. Each day, spend a few minutes noting down your thoughts and responses to the various things that you have had to deal with, especially the tough situations. Setting time aside for reflection and processing can increase your understanding of your internal emotions. This can help you to adjust your behaviour for more positive outcomes.

And remember

Some leaders think that being in touch with your emotions is just 'soft stuff' that they can ignore. Frankly for some it is scary. However, understanding and showing emotional intelligence is fundamental to being a leader. One of the most important questions any leader can ask is not 'How do others experience me?', but 'How do they experience themselves when they are experiencing me?' This gets to the heart of being a leader. After a meeting or conversation with you, do people leave feeling uplifted and energised or drained, anxious and demoralised? Are you an energy sink or an energy radiator? (See the section on Being an energy radiator, p. 12.)

To be effective as a leader of smart people you have to understand how your behaviour affects their emotions – the impact you have on them – and then to have a reasonable understanding of how those emotions will affect their behaviour. The good news is that emotional intelligence can be learnt and developed, and time invested in developing it is always time well spent.

Impostor syndrome

Impostor syndrome – that feeling that we are simply not good enough – is a relatively common phenomenon in populations of smart people. Studies suggest it impacts around 70 per cent of us at one stage or another. Deep down, every leader knows that things change; mistakes happen and things need to be reworked or rectified when they have not gone according to plan.

Smart leaders draw strength from knowing that none of us is the 'full package', and recognise that they also suffer from the occasional crisis of confidence. However, they need to have a *realistic* confidence most of the time, based on an understanding of their own capabilities and strengths, technical and interpersonal, and self-knowledge about where they need help. They realise that the world is too complex and fast-moving to be fully on top of everything all the time. Their key is being alert to these changes and trusting in their own skills and capabilities to be able to tackle them effectively.

Example

Mary was delighted when her Head of Research invited her to submit a paper based on her PhD to present at an upcoming global conference. As she was preparing to meet the Head of Research to discuss the conference, it dawned on her that the audience would contain several of the world's best in her field. This was a level of exposure to which she was completely unaccustomed. Whilst she was elated at the prospect, her heart began to beat faster as she imagined how some of the audience might react.

The 'sinking' feeling in the pit of her stomach increased as the time for the meeting drew nearer. Her eyes alighted upon the paperweight that was a memento of her PhD presentation. She was instantly reminded of a similar anxiety – thinking she was not up to the task – when she was completing her PhD submission and ahead of the viva that followed. She dug deeper, reflecting on what had got her through these situations in the past and how she might use what she had done before to help deal with this new challenge. She made notes to pull in one of her junior researchers and asked her assistant to gather reference pieces from others who would be presenting alongside her. As a final thought she blocked out time before meeting with her boss in order to ensure she had everything ready. Pushing back her chair, she realised that her mind had stopped racing and her blood pressure had reverted to normal. It was going to be a successful presentation. Taking a step back and reflecting on how she had used her strengths and skills to overcome anxieties about her ability to deliver in the past offered her a route map to face this new challenge, no matter how daunting it had at first seemed.

Do this

→ Be realistic

Stop imagining that things are worse than the real situation. Make your assessments of situations and circumstances grounded in reality and ask colleagues or people you trust. Do they see things the same way? What is their analysis of the situation? Why might their view be different to yours?

→ Check your history

Reflect on where you have had to deal with similar situations in the past. How did you do so? What skills and capabilities did you use? What did you learn from them? The better your awareness of your own strengths, the more likely it is that you will find ways of resolving present issues.

→ Be vulnerable

Share your concerns with your people. Your people are smart; they don't expect you to know *everything*. They *know* that you don't know everything and they will want to help you. Vulnerability is OK. Copping out is not, nor is ploughing on regardless. It's OK to be unsure from time to time; give yourself that permission.

→ Trust your team

Building high-performing teams gives you additional resources on which to draw. Strong, diverse teams bring together different skills and perspectives. Share problems with them and ask for their input and advice.

→ Stop comparing

Don't compare yourself to others. How others have dealt with situations that might seem similar to yours is not a good comparison. True, there may be some overt similarity and even things to learn. But humans are uniquely individual beings, and how others make sense of their world and view their problems will not be the same for you. They also have different skills, knowledge and experience to bring to bear. Stop comparing yourself with others and look instead to your own past and what you have learnt from your missteps and your successes.

→ Focus on what you're good at

Focus on making the most of your skills and talents, the things you're especially good at. Relate those skills to your successes in the past and draw strength from that. You were able to do it before; there is probably no reason why you cannot be successful now. But stay open to offers of help too.

→ Check out your 'mind talk'

What are you saying to yourself in your head? Are things really that bad? Remove the extremes and replace them with the moderate and realistic. Things are invariably not as bad as they might seem.

→ See mistakes as mis-takes

See a mistake for what it is – a signal – and do something different as a result. Mistakes are part of the learning process and simply a sign that a course of action has not worked out as expected. Things are neither inherently good or bad, just more or less effective.

→ Stop attributing success or failure to luck or unseen forces

Luck or fate, or however you phrase it, should have no place in your thinking. Luck is simply being attuned to circumstances and realising the probabilities that can be exploited.

→ Show self-confidence

Talk straight, hold yourself upright, make sure your posture looks confident to others. Being self-confident is an attribute that people expect in their leaders. It is attractive to other people. It is the self-assurance that comes from being able to say to oneself, honestly, I know I am able to do X, Y or Z.

→ Pretend you are good at it anyway

Rehearse confident behaviour; walking tall, speaking clearly and firmly, listening intently, controlling nervous mannerisms, breathing deeply. By acting in a certain manner we assume the characteristics of how we are behaving. It is the old Socratic idea that by acting virtuously we become virtuous. To mis-paraphrase the Greek master, if we act confidently we become confident.

And remember

Impostor syndrome can be triggered when something does not go well or we receive negative feedback (feedback that is often poorly delivered as well). Keeping that one piece of negative feedback in its place is important. If it was poorly delivered then assume good intention; someone was trying to help and just delivered the message poorly.

And remember that this one piece of feedback is probably one piece amongst many positive ones. An ability to see the world as it really is comes from taking time out to stop, reflect, think some more and check to make sure our mental models of the world really reflect that reality. A balanced view is a source of confidence and realism. People want to follow and trust leaders who, while being human and authentic, see the world clearly and show confidence in their decisions and direction.

Listening

It is a curious thing that probably the most important skill for any leader, and especially the leader of smart people, is one that is rarely taught. It is a skill in which most people think they are already proficient: how to listen. The skill of listening – really listening, empathically, and being able to demonstrate to the other person that you have heard and understood them – is invaluable. This goes beyond what is being said, and includes how it is being said and the intended meaning: listening 'between the lines' for why these things are being said at this time in this way.

Being able to listen one-on-one is great, but to whom are you listening? To lead smart people successfully you need to know when to bring others into the conversation, and how to show that you have been listening to the feeling of the entire group. These judgement calls go beyond simply being able to listen one-on-one. They involve understanding how the conversation is heard by others and the impact it may have on them. Leaders of smart people know that how they manage these interactions is important because hearing a wide range of views produces better solutions.

Example

As managing partner of his firm, Johan had ambitious goals which included the acquisition of a smaller firm with complementary services. He shared his initial ideas with his immediate inner circle of confidant(e)s who were also in broad agreement. Together they worked up a plan to share the ideas with an increasing number of small groups of partners in the firm, in part to build a base of support but also to understand what the difficulties or issues might be.

As a partnership there were, of necessity, many meetings with partners to agree the terms of the deal and how to raise necessary capital. Some felt the acquisition might take the firm's eye off the ball and were vocal in their opposition, but the groundwork done by the smaller groups and coalitions they had built paid off. Johan knew there was now a body of support in the partnership; it was just not being heard. He made a point of personally speaking with many of his partners, especially the opinion-formers. He drew people out by reflecting what they had said – word for word with some, paraphrasing and summarising with others, or simply reflecting back the sentiment he had discerned.

At the partners' meeting to vote on the acquisition, Johan listened patiently and sincerely to the objections. Again, he reflected back, paraphrased and summarised to make sure his partners knew that they had been heard. He also made a specific point of inviting the quieter members to contribute. By the time Johan said 'Let's take stock' it was clear the mood of the majority was in favour.

By listening carefully to his partners – both those with objections and the quieter ones – Johan had a clear view of the feeling in the partnership. The fact that he was seen to be listening meant that everyone felt their views had been considered and was committed to making sure that the acquisition was a success.

Do this

→ **Get rid of the distractions**
Focus on the other person. Smart people know when they are being listened to. If you are truly listening you cannot also be formulating your next question or writing words down. We pick up micro-signals of behaviour that are more or less uncontrollable. So stay focused on the whole person in front of you. Let them know, by your behaviours, that they have your full attention.

→ **Keep the conversation going**
Don't ask questions unless you want to change the direction of the conversation. Saying 'Go on', 'Tell me more', 'And then', 'And' will encourage the other person to keep speaking. And if they stop, don't rush to fill the gap; just keep listening.

→ **Be still, in the moment**
Keep still and show you are paying attention. Nod, raise your eyebrows at the right time. Broadcast signals that indicate you are listening. When you are listening, adopt the listening position: lean slightly forward and keep still; head slightly on one side; hand loosely placed on your thighs.

→ **Don't leak**
People usually, and unintentionally, 'leak' behaviour. They tap, fidget or give off other behaviours that give clues to their internal state. Focusing on the other person and what is going on in the 'here and now' will enable you to give signals that you are listening.

→ **Be careful when asking questions**
Ask open questions when you want to dive deeper into a topic. Use 'Who?', 'What?', 'When?', 'Where?' and 'How?' But beware using 'Why?' in this context: it can imply criticism or that you are seeking a justification. It might elicit a defensive response or start to close down what might otherwise be a free offering of information.

→ **Be comfortable with silence**
Increase your tolerance for dealing and being comfortable with silence. It is a great way of eliciting more information. Smart people are more likely to choose their language carefully to express points, especially ones that may be contentious or awkward; learn to give them space and not to fill every second with your own voice.

→ **Use the silence**
You don't have to talk all the time. It is perfectly OK as a leader to just sit quietly. Your smart people will usually have lots to say. The only choice you have to make as a leader is whether to direct the conversation or not; in most cases not. Let the speaker tell their story, in their words, their way. But do seek clarification.

→ **Master the techniques of reflecting, repeating, paraphrasing**
Reflecting means playing back what you have just heard with your best attempt at the emotional context you have discerned. Use this when there is a break in the conversation or you want to make sure you have understood the meaning.

Repeating means just that: repeating word for word what was said. Use it to demonstrate that you have heard exactly what was said.

Paraphrasing means using *your* words to play back what you have heard. Use this when summarising or when you want to 'punctuate' a conversation or move on to the next part of the story or next steps.

→ **Stop making notes**
Don't make notes; just focus completely on the sounds entering your ears. If you are supposed to be listening, listen. If you do need to make a note, ask the other person if it is OK to do so, but be careful about affecting the flow of the conversation. Make your note and then put the pen down and refocus.

→ **Be clear on what you are listening for**
Listen for the accent and emphasis on certain words and phrases. You are listening for emotions: real or implied. You are listening for emphasis: what is being stressed or repeated, and why.

→ **Listen widely**
Know when you need to expand your conversation. Who else do you need to hear from? A key listening skill is observing when to bring in other people who can add, challenge and provide a different or supporting perspective. Smart leaders work with others to help them make the right decisions.

→ **Choose when to listen or lead**
Learn when to listen and when to lead. Sometimes intervening to help take the discussion forward is the right thing to do. At other times, resisting

the pressure to direct things because we know the answer or the way forward is the right choice. Good leaders tend to make these judgements more subtly and appropriately.

And remember

Listening and hearing are not the same thing. Check that you really are listening deeply and not just using the time to think about what you are going to say next. Most of the time what we are actually listening for is a gap in the conversation so that we, smart people, can figure out the next smart question to ask or smart point to make. Learn to become comfortable with two things: not knowing all the answers, and allowing silence to do its work. Really listening to another person takes discipline and choosing the right time not to talk.

Leaders work through groups and teams so choosing to whom one listens – and when – is important. Your people want to know that their views and ideas have been heard and acknowledged, even if those ideas may not be used. Smart people thrive in the company of other smart people, so knowing when and how to include them, skilfully bring them in, make sure they are heard by their colleagues, and manage their contributions is important because of the overall effect it has on the team as well as the individuals.

Management

It may seem paradoxical in a leadership book to be writing about day-to-day management. But part of the role of being a successful leader in professional environments also means making sure the management work actually gets done. Managing is different from leading. Managing is about organising, planning, coordinating: making sure the bills are sent, the cash collected, staff appraisals completed, and internal policies and procedures adhered to. This may sound dull, and far less glamorous and important than leading a proposal team or solving a difficult client issue, but it is a crucial function. And this is especially the case where the seemingly routine and bureaucratic are seen as necessary evils that often take second place to the interesting technical aspects of the work.

It is important to remember that your credibility amongst your people is partly dependent on how you model the behaviours you expect of them. So, if you ignore the routine, so will your teams. It is also worth remembering that you are appraised and recognised for your ability to manage, raise and collect revenue as well as your technical and leadership skills. Whatever the level at which you're operating, you will always be a fee earner.

Example

Dario was one of the founders of the start-up and a gifted software wizard. His technical work, in terms of both his in-house duties and well-respected peer-reviewed papers, was one of the reasons that the business had no trouble in raising finance from its backers. However, board meetings were starting to become a problem, as Dario was frequently absent, working on interesting technical developments he considered more important than reporting on progress. This was compounded when it became obvious that the finances for Dario's department were receiving scant attention, with recruitment, advertising and travel budgets heavily overspent. Questions from the Finance Controller were ignored and meetings postponed.

The HR Director arranged to meet with Dario and had a frank, heart-to-heart conversation where she explained the full impact of Dario's single-minded focus on the technical problems. It was clear that Dario had not realised the second and third levels of impact that his behaviour was having. Over time, the HR Director and Dario established a routine, delegating key tasks to his team to help with the work. She also arranged for the IT Manager to improve the functionality of Dario's equipment. The finance team rallied around to help him develop his budgets – and stick to them. Dario had always added substantial technical value to the business but now investors were seeing him as a much more rounded business executive. He had realised that he needed to take more seriously the routine tasks that were crucial for the business to thrive and assumed proper responsibility for making sure that someone in his team was tasked with getting them done.

Do this

→ Change the way you think about routine tasks

Recognise that this is important work. Keep reminding yourself that it's vital for the long-term health of your business and give it due time and attention.

→ Realise that some of this stuff you have to do yourself

Only do yourself the routine administrative work that you have to do. Other tasks can be delegated, but don't forget that the responsibility for checking that it is done correctly and on time lies with you. Your team needs to see you model the behaviour you expect of them.

→ Work with your organisation's business cycle

Use your organisation's business cycle to establish a routine. For example, expense claims on Tuesdays; client billing every Friday; staff performance reviews completed by 30 June. That these things need to be done is no surprise. Build 'mini-routines' to clear the administrative work and build this time into your overall schedule and link it, sensibly, to your firm's annual cycle.

An early starter? Carve out time early to get it done. Regular meetings? Schedule some extra management time. This may sound counter-intuitive, but clearing the management work leaves time – and a clearer mind – for the rest of the job.

→ Talk to colleagues or partners who are good at this

Every firm has leaders who are role models. Who in your organisation has their book of business or budgets firmly under control? Their billings and cash collection always on budget, high levels of recovery and low levels of work in progress? Appraisals always done on time? Talk to them and ask them how they do it.

→ Really understand how your firm's systems work and interrelate with each other

The finance, marketing and HR people in your firm love to spend time with the leaders of the business. They like it even more when those leaders show a real interest in the functional work they do for the firm. Enlist their help. Get your functional specialists to explain the stuff they do and crucially *why* it is done the way it is. Their advice and counsel will not only offer a better solution; they may even be able to take some of the work away or help you to get it done more easily. These people will have trained in their respective functions and will be good at it. So make sure that you, the team, the department, firm or organisation use their expertise and advice.

→ **Teach your juniors why the management work is so important**

Show your people how to do the various jobs and help them to get the jobs done. Explain why it is so important and must be done well. Make it very clear that this is an essential part of their role. By helping you and building a broader understanding of how the business operates, they are also developing themselves.

And remember

Make no mistake, getting the management part of the job done on time and accurately is a key part of leading smart professionals. You have to be able to blend the execution of your management and leadership responsibilities. As the leader, your behaviour as a role model is vitally important. So make sure more routine administrative tasks are taken seriously and done well to set a good example. If you stop leading, the business is unlikely to grow and will atrophy. If you stop managing, you jeopardise profitability and potentially increase your risk profile. The management parts of the role may not be glamorous. But they are essential tasks and need your attention, energy and, crucially, your time. You can't run a business without cash and you can't run a business without managing it. It may never be as exciting as developing the business or doing the technical work. But building a routine that enables you to get the management done as part of your leadership is essential. Ignore it at your peril.

Multitasking

Multitasking – doing more than one thing at once – has often been seen as the key to executive success; the way to get more done, more quickly. Those who can multitask are supposed to be winners and those who can't – well …

For busy leaders juggling the workload of producing, managing and leading, multitasking is inevitable. The interrupted phone call, an instant message interrupting the drafting of a report are simply facts of life. However, there is a difference between interruptions that crop up in the course of a day's work and initiating them ourselves. The simple fact is that multitasking is inefficient. Both knowledge work and leadership benefit from periods of focused, uninterrupted attention.

The good news is that humans *can* and *do* multitask; we drink tea and watch the television; we cook and speak – all examples of multitasking. But there is bad news too. Humans cannot multitask when the multitasking involves attempting more than one *cognitive* task, like writing an email and reconciling a spreadsheet; creating a presentation and holding a telephone call about a negotiation. For cognitive processing, the human brain is a linear processor: it does *one thing at a time*. So, by attempting two or more cognitive tasks at the same time, your brain simply rapidly switches between the two tasks and uses more time and fuel to get reorientated to the needs of the tasks. Research has repeatedly proven that the time needed to complete *both* tasks takes significantly longer. Smart leaders in knowledge-rich environments know that multitasking does not provide the answers it might at first seem to offer.

Example

Jo really stood out amongst her colleagues. They used to laugh at the way she diligently focused and allocated time to her to-do lists and managed her schedule with her time management system. They marvelled that she sat and concentrated on conference calls without reading emails and resolutely refrained from using her mobile phone to check her incoming email during meetings.

But the biggest surprise for her colleagues came at bonus time. It was apparent that, by any metric, Jo's productivity and deliverables were way ahead of target. She even managed to get home at a sensible hour in the evenings. When questioned about how she did it, Jo simply felt that she used her time more efficiently than her colleagues. In fact, her ability to focus uninterrupted on individual knowledge-rich tasks in sequence gave her a competitive advantage over others who were attempting the impossible juggling act of attempting more than one cognitive task at a time.

Do this

→ **Stop trying**
Recognise that trying to multitask is a habit you need to break. It will require you to be disciplined with yourself. Be mindful and catch yourself when you start to slip. Awareness is crucial and being aware of the temptation is key.

→ **Resist the temptation**
Remove the things that cause you the distraction. Shut your computer screen down during meetings and conference calls unless you are referring to material relating to the meeting. Switch your mobile phone off or to silent – or better still put it out of sight. And *leave it alone*.

→ **Focus and concentrate on the task in hand**
Make clear choices about what is the most important task at any one time. The key thing is choosing the right things to do. Pareto was right: what are the 20 per cent of tasks that will give you 80 per cent of results and therefore need your complete attention? Allocate uninterrupted time to complete these.

→ **Choose your work location with care**
For important tasks, consider finding a location where you will be out of the way and can focus.

→ **Be realistic about the consequences**
Ignore the source of your interruptions. Yes, really. It is highly unlikely that anyone will cancel a contract if you fail to ring them back immediately or respond to an email for 30 or 60 minutes.

→ **Stop making excuses**
Smart people find a thousand and one ways to justify poor behaviour. See your excuses for what they are: justification of poor work habits. Multitasking is not making you more efficient or effective.

→ **Catch your juniors**
Watch out for your team members who are trying to multitask – and stop them. Make it clear you do not value the behaviour and are worried about the risks they may be creating by their partial attention to the issues with which they are dealing.

→ Become 'virtuous'

When it makes sense, make a point of letting your colleagues know when you are switching off your source of interruptions. Make use of out-of-office and voice message facilities.

→ Be vigilant

Stay alert to the way you are working and stop yourself slipping back into habitual patterns. Recognise that you are not only fighting a personal habit – you are likely surrounded by others who are also displaying bad habits. Don't let them suck you back in.

And remember

This section is necessarily short – the advice, simply, is be very careful when you are tempted to try and do two thinking tasks at the same time. Attempting cognitive multitasking is invariably inefficient and counter-productive; overall, it usually takes longer to complete the tasks.

As a leader it also sets a poor example; as with other issues, you need to show what good behaviour looks like. There is a time to focus and be seen to be focusing, especially on non-urgent but important tasks. If your team sees you trying to multitask – not paying attention on conference calls because you are checking email, for example – they will follow your lead. By your very behaviour you set a precedent for what is acceptable and appropriate. Do not encourage multitasking.

Presentations

How did you feel when you saw Steve Jobs launching a new Apple product? He sold himself, his knowledge, his presence, his product and service. It appeared effortless and his message was delivered simply so everyone could engage with and understand it. Everyone looked forward to his next event. He was judged through his presentation skills.

Presenting is part of professional life and, unlike Steve Jobs, you may have to make the dullest of technical subjects sound interesting and accessible. Smart people hugely benefit by presenting with confidence and clarity to staff, clients, partners, investors and, at times, the public. However, it's a skill that even some seriously smart people can struggle with, no matter how much they shine in a one-on-one setting. The good news is that smart people judge other smart people as they judge themselves and, so long as the intellect is there, they can be very forgiving. The even better news is that presenting is a skill like any other that can be learnt and developed with practice and experience.

Example

Pierre was a senior manager in an accounting firm. The firm was offering presentation skills training to improve the quality of the partners' 'pitch' presentations and Pierre volunteered to attend if there were any last-minute cancellations. When he was offered a place, he cleared his schedule and duly attended. The training was lively and covered structure, content and delivery with opportunities to practise in front of other course attendees.

Six months later, Pierre was in New Delhi attending an international conference with the firm's Hong Kong Managing Partner. It was an exciting and intimidating crowd of highly influential, smart movers and shakers in the sector. Pierre felt out of his comfort zone – and, in truth, a little in awe of the event and his surroundings.

On the second morning, the Hong Kong Managing Partner volunteered Pierre to stand in as a speaker on the last day – one of the guest speakers was delayed and his colleague thought Pierre's involvement would be good exposure for the firm. Pierre felt nervous at the prospect, but realised it was time to make use of his training. It all came flooding back. He realised he did know how to structure and organise content, to use his voice and body, and he threw himself into his preparations with lots of help from the Managing Partner. The talk to a big crowd of experts was certainly a baptism of fire, but Pierre's training stood him in good stead and his presentation was considered a success.

When Pierre got back to London everyone seemed to know about his exploits – including his somewhat aloof Senior Partner who came to his office to congratulate him. His burgeoning reputation for presenting helped him to stand out amongst his peers and he was regularly offered career-enhancing speaking opportunities. Pierre's training had helped him to understand that presentation skills can be learnt and developed and gave him the practical tools and techniques he needed to perform under pressure.

Do this

→ **Prepare and set out the scope and depth of what you are going to say**
Preparation is the key to presenting success. Frame the topic and content as a journey, plotting the start point, the steps along the way, and the destination. Find out what the audience already know about the topic; this will inform you about how much technical jargon to use and what you may need to explain. Keep your message to three points or a maximum of five. Ask yourself the questions 'What's in it for them?' and 'What would I need to know from their perspective?'

→ **Open with impact**
First impressions set the tone for the presentation. Give the audience a 'hook', something that piques their interest and is memorable. This could be a stark highlight, a surprise graphic, or some form of dramatic device or visual prop.

→ **Decide on the media you will use**
Avoid death by PowerPoint and never simply read from notes or slides. Your audience is perfectly capable of reading. Smart people are measured by how well they can strip away complexity and technical points so that they can be easily grasped and understood. Think about how the audience normally communicates and use that to guide your media. Would they use flow charts, statistics, props, pictures? Try connecting with a medium that resonates with them so they can absorb the message more quickly.

→ **Use your own style**
Be authentic. Use your voice and your body so that you are not trying to be something you are not. If you can be informal – sitting on a table or next to some of the audience – and that is appropriate for your material, then do that. If you need to be more formal, speak to the back of the room. Check if your audience speaks in your mother tongue. If not, moderate your speed and select your vocabulary carefully. Adjust to your audience. Above all, look at the audience, smile and use open gestures.

Be 'light' when it will help

Use appropriate humour and wit to lighten the tone. Making relevant, 'in the here and now' comments, or referencing a previous speaker, can really help. For example, 'In the next hour and a half I'd like to cover X, Y and Z, but I can see from looking at you it would be better if this was all done in under an hour – so let's go for that.' Be wary of telling jokes that can so easily offend or backfire.

Deal with nerves

If you are not nervous, something is not right. Use coping techniques such as taking three deep breaths, drinking a glass of water, or transferring the attention to the audience by throwing out a question. The answer can be an excellent strategy to display your knowledge.

Make sure it all works …

Rehearsal is another key to presenting success. It will help you to refine your content and check your timing.

On the day itself, try to check out the facility and make sure you are familiar with any technology. Do film clips play when they should? Is the sound loud enough? How will you enter and exit the stage?

Close with impact

Summarise your key messages. Always keep to time or even finish slightly before time. If smart people are interested, they will want to ask questions so allow adequate time. They will want to test the speaker's depth of knowledge and may well be thinking of him/her as a potential adviser.

And remember

Many smart people are fearful of presenting, of freezing on the spot or being exposed by a difficult question. But like so many other leadership skills, presenting can be learnt and developed with practice. The essential thing is for you to know your stuff and not to try to blind the audience with your science. Then the key is preparation, preparation, preparation – and practice, practice, practice. Try asking a trusted colleague to give honest feedback. Even better, get them to ask questions that might come up, so you can practise answering. Remember to make it real so your listeners can engage and relate to it. Smart people like real-world stories, especially if the links and parallels are made clear for them.

Juggling roles of leading, producing and managing

A key issue for the leader of smart people is the basis of their authority. Smart people often have little regard for formal organisational authority, but they do pay a lot of attention to the technical or professional expertise of their leaders. This is not to say that they expect their leaders to be technically the best in the world. But they do expect their leaders to understand the technicalities of the work and have something to offer at this level. In short, smart people expect their leaders to be able to add something substantive to their own endeavours. This situation is particularly acute in the world of professional services such as the law, medicine, accounting, consulting or science.

This is different to many corporate organisations where promotion up the corporate ladder means that leaders become more removed from the detailed day-to-day work of their departments, but instead become experts in getting things done inside the organisation. Their technical knowledge is superseded by detailed expertise in the organisation's systems, processes and political dynamic. In other words, the nature of their 'technical' knowledge changes with the promotions.

To maintain their credibility, leaders of smart people need to be able to be producers (i.e. doing the technical work) as well as managing and leading their teams. This can be tough, but managing the demands of this multiplicity of roles is essential if the leader is to retain the respect and trust of their teams. Being able to balance these competing needs requires absolute clarity of purpose, self-awareness and smart time management.

Example

No one was surprised when Marcia, an expert in tax transfer pricing, was promoted to lead an important team at her firm in Buenos Aires. She had established herself as the 'go-to person' for advice by the firm's top clients. She was acknowledged as a leading expert in her field, even by her competitors. She was at the top of her game.

But nothing had prepared Marcia for the challenge of stepping up into a leadership role. For the first time, her relentless and successful focus on her technical area of expertise was under threat. She found herself frustrated by having to spend time doing things other than advising clients. She was struggling to connect with her team members and had begun to notice that they were avoiding her. What with her clients and the team, there was always too much to do and never enough time in which to do it. Marcia couldn't understand why she always seemed to feel exhausted and overwhelmed.

It was a conversation with Rick, a colleague and friend who worked elsewhere in the business, that finally helped Marcia to make sense of what stepping up into a leadership role really means. After listening to Marcia's difficulties, Rick simply suggested that she could not keep working in the way she'd always done. Now that she had competing priorities, she would have to balance her own strategic goals with the needs of managing and leading her team – and to make time for everything, she would have to make hard choices about what to focus on herself and when to enlist the help and support of others.

For a high achiever like Marcia, it was hard to acknowledge that she couldn't simply do everything herself, that her technical expertise was not, on its own, enough and that her new role needed a different approach. But, in time and with the support from Rick and others, things began to improve. By acknowledging the challenge of playing multiple roles, and finding practical ways to manage her workload, Marcia's team came to value her as a leader able to share as well as deploy her still formidable technical expertise.

Do this

→ **Have a strategic agenda**
Identify your five to seven big priorities for the next 18 to 24 months. This is not a to-do list, but a list of the big things that are going to make a real difference to your unit's performance. Being clear about your direction and executing those priorities will help you to stay focused and operate at the strategic level leadership demands.

→ **Make time for managing and leading**
Avoid the siren call of getting deeply buried in the technical aspects of the work at the expense of everything else. Carve out time to lead the team as individuals and as a group as well as dealing with the necessary management tasks like organising, planning, coordinating. Above all, be a role model.

→ **Take very strict control of your time**
Allocate your time in line with your overriding priorities, as set out in your agenda. Be tough with yourself; you need to exercise self-discipline and stick to your priorities.

→ **Don't chase omniscience**
You can't be great at everything. Focus on the unique value you can add and work with the team to share the load. Figure out what you can do that the rest of the team cannot and make sure you add it.

→ **Extend your networks 1**
Seek contacts outside the usual subjects with whom you normally work. Reach out to peers, colleagues, talent wherever it exists in the organisation. Find ways of enlisting their help and support in the service of your agenda – can they offer advice, a viewpoint, a connection to someone else? If your agenda is interesting and exciting, other people will want to help and get involved.

→ **Extend your networks 2**
Seek help, advice and guidance from outside your organisation too. Talk to your external mentors, peers in non-competing organisations, external advisers and consultants. They too will have views and ideas or contacts and knowledge that may help you achieve your objectives.

→ **Use tasks for several purposes**
Find ways of using one task for more than one purpose in the pursuit of your objectives. A trip back from a meeting with a junior colleague is an opportunity to give them feedback or to ask them to give you feedback. An overseas meeting with a client is also an opportunity to spend an extra day meeting colleagues in that overseas office and sharing the news from your office. Being creative with the way you allocate and execute your tasks means you get more done in the same space of time, grows your team members and consequently the overall capability of your part of the organisation.

→ **Be opportunistic**
Look out for serendipitous events that can work in your favour. Chance meetings in the elevator, seeing someone at the water cooler or coffee machine or lunch queue. Use these instances to further your agenda: perhaps a quick progress check, a word of encouragement or feedback, maybe you need clarity on a point or to make a slight change. These moments are efficient ways of communicating, but you need to be alert to the opportunities when they present themselves.

→ **Review your own working habits**
Take some time to consider: Are you still working in the same way that you have always done? True, it will have been part of what has made you successful, but are there working practices that need to be revised? Changed? Stopped? New tools, software or technology that you should be learning to use?

And remember

This multiplicity of roles is not a mere semantic invention; it has very real consequences for the mindset of the leader of smart people. They are constantly battling the conflicting demands of technical work with managing and leading; with immediate crises and the longer-term demands of the business; of maintaining technical proficiency whilst running the business and at the same time trying to learn for 'the manage and lead'. It is a situation that can often lead to cognitive overload.

Learning how to accommodate these conflicting demands is, in our experience, what separates the really successful leaders of smart people from those who just get by and do an OK job. Recognising the phenomenon, and creating personal coping strategies like the ones noted above, is absolutely vital for success.

Resilience

The present-day leader of smart people lives in a pressurised world: non-stop demands from clients, technology-enabled 24/7 contact with the entire globe; responsibilities inside the organisation; requests for help from colleagues – and all the while trying to maintain some semblance of a personal life.

Resilience is the ability to deal with continuous pressure and keep performing at a high level over extended periods of time, and in conditions of ambiguity and uncertainty. It is about your capacity to focus your agenda, how you use your time and work with your teams. Our experience shows that those leaders who consistently outperform tend to take good care of themselves. This helps them build capacity, reserves of time, health and energy that allow them to respond when crises or opportunities present themselves. When leading smart people, those demands are ever more acute because of the intellects with which you are interacting on an hourly basis.

Most of us just drop into a routine and don't take the time to stop, rethink and reflect. But reflecting on how we have used our time, on our meetings and interactions, is a practice that every leader should undertake. Only by reflecting can we take the time to process and make sense of the world. Time out allows our physiology to rest and recharge. Stopping is difficult but it's especially important when we are feeling under constant pressure, a hamster on a wheel. Build time in your diary to so do.

Example

Marius was a senior executive in a large international business. His responsibilities required a lot of travel and the constant juggling of a demanding workload of both internal management and leadership tasks as well as servicing an important customer base. He had recently witnessed one of his close peers experiencing what can only be described as burnout; after years of overwork and the breakdown of his marriage, he had finally hit the buffers.

On yet another international flight, Marius was reflecting on that colleague and why, although he had a similarly demanding workload, he seemed able to cope better with its pressures. The answer seemed to be surprisingly simple: discipline and a clear sense of priorities. For Marius, these started with his personal well-being so that he could look after his family, then his responsibilities as an elder in his faith community, and then his work responsibilities. His mantra was 'the best investment is in your health'. Wherever he was in the world, he maintained a routine of exercise; he was a long-distance runner and always made sure he kept fit. He enjoyed a glass of wine but ate and drank sensibly. He invariably found time to read a book a week. Like many of us, he could be hard on himself, but he also tried to cut himself some slack and keep moving forward.

Marius attributed his resilience to being vigilant about his purpose in life and that drove his sense of priorities. Having that clarity enabled him to achieve an accommodation between his different priorities and achieve a sense of balance that worked for him.

Do this

→ **Check your mind talk**
Become conscious of what you are saying to yourself. We all make assumptions, often spending hours replaying the 'he said, she said' dialogue in our heads. We call this mind talk – and yes, everybody does it. It is not usually productive. Our thoughts and emotions are simply warning signals. Wasting energy trying to compute the myriad of permutations that can happen in human interactions is pointless. If you do feel the need to try and control it, try drawing out the options on a one-page mind map or spider diagram or some other graphic device that works for you. And then leave it alone; you have mapped out the options. Now decide and act. Move forward.

→ **Watch your language**
Be clear with your language. When you are planning a response, start by removing the 'coulds', 'shoulds' and 'oughts' from the way you describe things to yourself. Replace them with new, neutral and realistic descriptors of the situation. How we phrase things affects how we think about them.

For negative 'mind talk' stop yourself and use positive words and phrases. Words create thoughts. The simple act of bringing the unconscious into the conscious and realising what we are saying to ourselves is the first step. Then evaluating the circumstances in a realistic manner is incredibly empowering.

→ **Get your health in order**
Do you have regular medical check-ups? Do you exercise regularly? If the answer to these questions is no, get a check-up and listen to your physician. If you haven't exercised recently, speak to your doctor or fitness centre about establishing a regime that works for you and your lifestyle. Don't overdo it at the beginning. Set a time and pace that are good for you. You need to establish this as a habit – which can be tough. But persevere.

→ **Diet matters too**
Take control of how you are fuelling your system. Do you really need that starter, that dessert, that extra glass of wine? Are you drinking enough

water? Take sensible steps and watch your weight. If you need help, see a dietician and make the recommended changes. Remember, with a constant round of client entertaining and business development activities, the opportunity to over-participate is ever present.

→ Mix with optimistic people

We are influenced by the moods of the people with whom we associate. Choose the people with whom you spend your time carefully. You cannot completely avoid the cynical and the negative but, on balance, positive optimistic people are better for your health.

→ Take action

Probably the most important thing to do is to take action. If you are feeling under pressure, or not sure what to do, take the first step. And remember to take another step the following day. Building, or rebuilding habits – whether they are about exercise, diet or the way we talk to ourselves – takes time.

And remember

When work pressure mounts, often the first things to fall by the wayside are personal interests such as exercise or hobbies, and diet. We may start to pay less attention to those who are close to us as work eats further into time spent with family and friends, and, if we aren't careful, work has become all of our existence. We have seen this pattern so many times over the years and the impact (albeit unintended) on families and loved ones is very hard.

The cause of this phenomenon in most professional and technical environments is very simply the nature of the work itself, which can be fun, challenging, interesting and all-absorbing. There is no simple remedy, but vigilance and discipline can go a long way to keeping some sort of balance – or more likely accommodation – of what a sensible routine and time allotment between work and home looks like. There can be no prescription as to what is the right way to allocate your time, but making sure that you give time to home and looking after yourself is of vital importance. Set a good example by making sure we work in order to live and not the other way round. There is no better way to build resilience.

Rivals and jealousy

Most organisations profess themselves meritocracies where the best ideas, skills and people rise to the top of the hierarchy. In professional environments of all fields, this is also true, making the leadership task of leading former peers and rivals for the position you have been asked to undertake potentially very tricky.

You still need to maintain strong working relationships with these former peers and rivals who may well feel that that they have been unjustifiably passed over. (See the section on Choosing when to step up and lead, p. 81.) They will inevitably question why they should now follow you as the new leader when they believe the role should rightfully have been theirs. This can often lead to jealousy, rivalry and negative behaviours which will need to be addressed – and sooner rather than later.

Example

Charles and Olivia were deputies to Johan, head of a scientific department in a high-tech manufacturing company. Although their responsibilities were different, they were peers, professional equals and, moreover, friends. Both had ambitions to lead the department themselves one day. One morning they both had their regular monthly review meetings with the department head, Olivia at 8.30 and Charles at 9.15.

Johan ushered Olivia to a seat and announced that he was being promoted to a new position and he intended to appoint Olivia as his successor. How did she feel about that? Did she want the job? Thrilled, Olivia agreed immediately and they began to discuss the handover: timing, communication, responsibilities etc. Most importantly, they talked about Charles. Johan said he intended to share the news with Charles immediately. What was Olivia to say? To do? Charles was an important part of the department and they couldn't afford to lose him.

As Olivia left Johan's office, she said to Charles 'Your turn – he's all yours. See you shortly.' And headed back to her office. She knew she had 45 minutes to decide what to do and say until Charles left his meeting. She caught Charles as he was returning. 'Can we speak?' she offered. 'I think we need to.' Charles replied in a neutral tone and they headed into an empty office with Olivia following.

Olivia checked what Johan had said to Charles and they arranged to have a detailed conversation about how to redraw the boundaries of their roles and their personal relationship, Olivia's initial plans and ideas, and how she wanted to keep Charles engaged and involved. It was the first of three meetings. The first worked out the emotions at play, the second the practicalities for the rest of the team and the department, and the third was about how they both wanted their relationship to work in future.

The candour and openness of their conversation, reliving their past joint successes, the times when they had collaborated to solve issues, and an exploration of what they were both looking for now, led to a seamless handover of power in the department. Charles's reputation was enhanced by the way he handled himself during the transition and nine months later he too was offered a department of his own in another part of the organisation.

Do this

→ **Test your assumptions**
Ask yourself: is there really an issue here? Or are you having an attack of impostor syndrome or a mild case of organisational paranoia? What is the data you have to work with? Collect it and evaluate it carefully. Be very clear on what it is that is causing you concern. Then ask yourself: is this something that really needs my time and attention?

→ **Be aware of your emotions**
Identify the emotions you are feeling and what is causing them. Are you angry? Hurt? Resentful? Feeling undermined or betrayed? Do not react in haste; pay attention to the feelings and decide what you need to remedy and replace what you are feeling with more positive and productive ones.

→ **Have courage**
Leadership is about acting. If you have a real issue, take the initiative, but always know that your actions are being scrutinised. Whatever you do, your actions must bear public scrutiny and justification.

→ **Clarify what you want**
Be very clear and intentional about the outcomes you are seeking. What do you want the other person to stop or start doing? Make sure you are dealing with behaviour and *not* personality. Telling someone they are negative or meddling is no good. What behaviour have you seen or experienced that you are seeking to address and modify?

→ **Seek a joint solution**
Always give the other person the benefit of the doubt and recognise they will have good reasons, at least from their perspective, for their behaviour. Ask what it is they want to achieve and use that as the basis for your ongoing relationship.

→ **Think about them**
Always consider how your action – or your inaction – will be viewed by the rest of the group or team. Try and view it as an outsider. Have you been firm, fair, friendly and proportionate?

> **Test your response**
Ask yourself, if our roles were reversed and I was treated in this way, would I respect the person who did it? Your job isn't to make sure everyone loves each other, but you do need mutual respect – which is especially important for smart people. You also need to find ways to earn respect as a leader.

> **Redefine relationships and boundaries**
Have one-on-one conversations with people who may need to have the 'boundaries' redrawn. The old adage 'Good fences make good neighbours' is especially important.

> **Be transparent**
When differentiating people for advancement, bonuses or other benefits, have very clear and transparent criteria. Under no circumstances ever compare people directly one to another. Smart people are often very competitive and do not react well to personal comparisons.

→ **Use your power and authority wisely**
Are you being measured, reasonable and proportionate? Check in with a trusted confidant(e) or mentor to make sure.

→ **Get yourself air cover**
Check in with your boss, not necessarily to get permission but to:
(a) make sure that they know what you are proposing to do;
(b) solicit their advice and counsel – there may be history of which you are unaware;
(c) make sure they will support you.
Do this *before* you take major steps such as initiating disciplinary action.

And remember

The way in which we deal with former peers and colleagues is another signature touchpoint for how leadership is perceived. Your former peers and colleagues, your new subordinates and your bosses will be taking an interest in how you manage this dynamic. Get it wrong and performance will drop. Get it badly wrong and you will lose talent. Get it right and everybody wins.

Take the time to understand how others are feeling and then respond appropriately. The key to getting it right is to make sure you are always seen to be putting the needs of the organisation, its clients and customers, and your own team first. And never, ever, forget that you have to exercise a duty of care towards those who have been affected by your promotion. Whatever the behaviour of others, you, at the very least, should do the right thing.

The time bind

Most leaders of smart people (and their teams) are time-poor. However, the successful leaders with whom we have worked are ruthless in how they allocate their time. They know time is their most valuable resource and the one that is absolutely fixed and cannot be increased.

Successful leaders remain equally sensitive to the wants and needs of clients, their demanding colleagues and the wider organisation. The key issue is how to focus and allocate your finite time for the infinite number of options and opportunities with which you are faced. There is an expectation that smart leaders can do this, so the sooner you get to grips with robust time-management strategies, the better. Specific focus is essential for effectiveness, efficiency and productivity – and less personal anxiety. So how can you deliver more to others and yourself?

Example

Will was at his practice group's partner retreat. Along with the senior management team, they were meeting to discuss a variety of initiatives to grow the business. As always, there were lots of ideas and opportunities to be aired and discussed.

Having considered the merits and demerits of each and after a process of prioritisation, the CEO looked to the group for volunteers to take the chosen initiatives forward. Will knew he was expected to contribute, but found himself avoiding the CEO's gaze and feeling resentful and exasperated that he was being asked to take on yet another piece of work. Eventually, when pushed about the actions he would undertake, he blurted out: 'What? Apart from running my practice, keeping the clients happy, finding new clients, doing the work, and reporting back to my partners, meeting targets, and running and expanding a practice team. Where do you expect me to find the time?'

The CEO called for a short break in the proceedings and took Will off to one side. She made clear to Will that he needed to step up and accept his share of the workload – with a commitment that she would help with his personal prioritisation. Later she met with Will to discuss how he might deliver on his actions from the meeting as well as getting everything else done. Crucially, Will had not been able to identify a few overriding, selected priorities that would drive his practice forward. She helped him develop an agenda; a short prioritised list of high-level objectives would act as a benchmark by which he could judge how to use his time.

With the clarity provided by a big-picture agenda, Will's working life was transformed. It offered a set of criteria to filter out less important activities, and helped him decide when to delegate or reprioritise, making room for the business development tasks from the retreat that were needed to fuel the firm's growth.

Do this

→ **Decide on the type of department or practice you want to lead and make sure it is 'on strategy'**

Be clear on what you want to be known for in the marketplace. Make sure your intentions are aligned to the overall strategy of the firm or business. Do you want to dominate a particular niche? A particular service line? When you have this clear, figure out which clients will want to buy your services and set about acquiring them.

→ **Determine five to seven overriding priorities**

Identify the few big things that will get you closer to the sort of department, team or organisation you want to lead. Is it a new client? Or type of work? A reputation-making project? Growing some new partners? The five overriding priorities are *not* 'to-do' tasks. They are your personal strategy: the big things that, when accomplished, will have moved you close to the sort of business you are wanting to lead. In contrast, your to-do list is your implementation plan of the many, many things that will need to be done in order to achieve the overriding priorities.

→ **Focus on your agenda and prioritise**

Allocate your time rigorously. Tasks that are urgent are often not important. Deal with the important *and* urgent things first. Allocate time to focus on your agenda and build in 'chaos time', the safety valve in your schedule to deal with the crises that will inevitably occur during the week.

→ **Check your ways of working**

Plan to acquire the skills and knowledge you need to implement your agenda. Smart people (like you) usually like to be busy; it makes for a sense of value and contribution. Sometimes we do things that are really no longer essential or could be done by others elsewhere. To make space for the new, these things should be delegated or discarded.

→ **Delegate more**

Enable, train and support your team. Delegating well requires time and investment, but it will free up time to focus on priority issues for the future. (See the section on Delegating, p. 106.) Delegation needs team members to have two things:

motivation and skills. Motivation can be enhanced with timely coaching conversations. Skills are built through teaching and repeated practice. Resist the temptation to do it all yourself.

→ Change your time blocks

Try blocking out time for tasks. Instead of big blocks of time, allocate yourself 15 or 20 minutes' *uninterrupted* time to complete a piece of work or a subtask. Then do something different for one or two minutes. Then return to another subtask. Check your productivity – is it better? Find out what your optimal time block is. How much can you actually achieve in 15 or 20 minutes with no distractions and highly focused effort?

→ Use time creatively

Use one task for more than one purpose. A trip back from a client is an ideal time to debrief with juniors about the meeting you have just attended. How did they view the meeting? Did they understand why you ran the conversation with the client as you did? Have the juniors take the notes for you. They will learn to understand what 'good' looks like.

→ Work when you are most productive

Figure out when you are most productive and build your schedule accordingly. Are you 'best' in the morning, afternoon or evening? The 'when' doesn't really matter, as long as you know. As far as you can, schedule your workload accordingly; be creative when you are at your best and carry out more routine tasks at other times. Try to match your work with the times when you are feeling most productive and most effective.

→ Manage your email

Build a filing system in your email that enables you to keep only active emails in your inbox. And then try and keep that down to a single screen. The old adage still applies: read it once and deal with it, delegate it or delete it!

→ Turn to-do lists into 'not-to-do' lists

Check your lists – and prune them rigorously. We all have to-do lists and they are useful; they help us get stuff out of immediate memory and into a place where we think we might have them under control. But how many of those things have been moved from one list to the next new list and then the next new list? If you are moving stuff forward repeatedly, it is either not important or not urgent – or both – so get rid of it.

→ **Manage your technology – don't let it manage you**
Use your technology to harness your energy by using the 'out of office' when on vacation – and not replying to email. By making it clear to your teams when you are unavailable – maybe putting it on your email footer? The message here is to use the technology to liberate you and not to imprison you. And making it clear to your teams that you expect them to do the same.

→ **Stop trying to multitask**
Find ways of protecting blocks of time, no matter how small, when you can focus on specific tasks. (See the section on Multitasking, p. 48.)

And remember

We cannot overstate how important it is to spend quality time and focus on building yourself an agenda. Decide on those five to seven overriding priorities you have for your business over the next 18 to 24 months, the things that will move your organisation to the next level.

Use those priorities as the filter for how you spend your time. There will be panics and emergencies for which you will have set aside contingency time, but deal with them as quickly as possible and then refocus your time on those key priorities. And remember: an agenda is not a to-do list.

2.
Leading the Team

Choosing when to step up and lead
Coaching
Credibility
Disruptors
Decision-making
Delegating
Empowerment and motivation
Feedback/feed-forward
Giving praise
Impact and presence
Having necessary conversations
Resolving conflict
Setting objectives
Team dynamics
Remote teams
Working with different cultures

Choosing when to step up and lead

Successful smart leaders seem to have the knack of knowing when things need to be done and choosing the right moment to start moving things forward. We are talking about those occasions when it would be easier to just let things go rather than take the tougher choice of actively stepping up to lead.

Leadership is about acting and getting things done. How you respond when those moments of choice present themselves is key. How well can you spot those occasions when that extra leadership is needed? And when those times come, are you prepared to go into a place where you may be vulnerable, exposed to your peers, and yet still be prepared to act for the betterment of your colleagues, clients and organisation? When the time comes, how good are you at marshalling your courage and choosing to take that step up to lead?

Example

Annette was heading to the third meeting of the task force to which she had been 'volunteered' by her department head. The last two had not been a total waste of time, but pretty close to it. 'There must be better ways of spending my time,' she had thought. As before, the discussion circled without conclusion and little progress was being made.

Annette looked around the group and realised she could either sit quietly or act to make things better for everybody. She started gently, 'Can I try to summarise where I think we are?' and offered a summary. Then she brought in a quiet member of the group and closed down one of the more vocal members. Before long, it was obvious to everyone that she had become the de facto leader of the meeting. After her final summary and the meeting had closed, a colleague tapped her on the shoulder as they left the room and said, 'We were all so relieved that you stepped in to take the lead; we were paralysed by not wanting to take a risk and going nowhere.'

Annette had rightly judged that something needed to happen to make the task force more than a time-wasting talking shop. And she realised that she herself had the power to take the initiative and act. By doing so, she chose the riskier, but ultimately more satisfying, path of showing leadership. At the next meeting, everyone involved was more motivated and engaged and the task force ultimately completed a body of work which garnered praise from the department head and beyond. Annette had learnt an important lesson about trusting her instincts, stepping up and showing active leadership.

Do this

→ **Behave authentically**

Look and behave in a manner that conveys to others that you believe in, and are committed to, whatever it is you are doing. Embody what you are saying. Remember, actions speak louder than words; and smart people seem to have a 'sixth sense' that detects inconsistencies fast and very accurately, in part due to the critical nature of their training and professional development. Leaders must behave in a way that is consistent with what they are espousing. Your team want to connect with a leader who they see as a 'real' person.

→ **Listen to your gut instinct**

When you are feeling that something needs doing, look around: are others looking bored, worried, frustrated? If so, it probably means you are not alone and something needs to be done. Do *not* usurp the designated leader. Instead, make suggestions that can help the situation improve. Offer a summary with a suggestion for a next step tacked on the end. Do a 'stocktake' of what things are being discussed and ask if these are concluded or how things might be actioned.

→ **Talk group 'process'**

Make a commentary on what is happening in the group at that moment in time. Observations though, not accusations. Things like 'We seem to be discussing this point without coming to a resolution. Can we move to a decision now?' Or if the discussion has been lengthy, offer a summary and possible way forward. Commenting on what is happening, in the here and now, is powerful. Is one person dominating the conversation? Would it be good to hear from other voices? These are all examples of talking about the group process: what is going on in the here and now of the group. When these conversations lead to action, it becomes leadership.

→ **Practise leadership**

Volunteer and put yourself in positions where you have to lead: a residents' association, parent–teacher association, office task forces or teams, anything that will give you the chance to move to the edge of your comfort zone. Make sure you take time out to review what you did and how it was received. Is there something here that can be repeated/used again in the future? The more you practise, the better you get and the easier it gets. Like most skills, leadership needs practice and learning.

→ Constantly ask yourself: what can I do …?

Ask yourself, what can I do to help us get to a result, or an even better result, faster? This will keep you focused on the result and how you are interacting with the group. Self-awareness of how we impact on others is key to successful leadership.

→ Identify when there are likely to be opportunities to lead

Work out your organisation's business cycle: budgeting and capital expenditure, planning, performance appraisals, bonuses and promotions, values awards etc. If you know when things are going to happen, you can be prepared for the opportunities that will occur. If you know when budgets are due, you can get yours prepared ahead of time. Appraisals/performance reviews coming up? Get ready, prepare thoroughly and make sure you meet deadlines. And don't forget the importance of modelling good behaviour.

→ Give leadership away

Ask other members of the team to do things and offer help to get them done. Helping others grow and develop is probably the most important job of the leader: growing more leaders for the organisation. One of the paradoxes of leadership is that giving away power and authority is how you develop others. It also builds your reputation as a leader, especially with smart people who don't really like being told what to do. One proviso: some things cannot be delegated and those only you, the leader, can do.

And remember

There are different ways of leading, and one size will never fit all situations. There is ordinary, everyday leadership, when things are progressing and it's clear what needs to be done and how. This is 'business as usual' leadership, when your role as leader should be 'lite' touches to ensure things are moving in the right direction. In these cases, get out of the way and let the people get on with things with minimal interference.

When things become more ambiguous, teams need more active leadership. This still means involving and listening. It also means stepping up and making sure the right decisions are made. This requires courage, skill, an ability to embrace the ambiguity and continue to function well, whilst being able to tolerate that state of ambiguity longer than others, all the while behaving authentically. These are the occasions when choosing to lead is risky. Your smart people will scrutinise your actions closely. But such leadership moments are often remembered and will be referred to in the future as a guide for how you react and lead in tricky situations.

Coaching

At its heart, real professionalism is about the exercise of judgement. It is associated with the application of a body of knowledge to specific client problems or issues and finding client-centred solutions. But judgement is a tricky thing to acquire and can only really be learnt from experience. This is why coaching is a vital tool in the world of leading smart people. It can accelerate the process of acquiring judgement and help to develop younger professionals. Leaders can also benefit from having a coach – someone to help them think through difficult issues and to keep developing their own capabilities.

Coaching, in our terms, is simply the process of helping people learn how to help themselves and other people. Smart people want to learn how to get better at their profession. So, in order to lead them you need to find subtle ways to help them learn. Probably the best way to do this is by coaching. As a leadership skill, coaching has wide-ranging applications – with your teams, your partners and clients. With clients, it also has the added benefit of making them more committed to a solution that they have been involved in creating.

Example

It was late on a Friday evening. Ashish – the team leader – was sitting near Meena, who was hunched over her computer typing sporadically. Clearly something was not going well. 'Oh, I'm glad you're here,' said Meena, 'Can you help me with this note for that new software client?'

Ashish started asking questions. What do we want to achieve over the next 20 minutes? And where shall we start? This was followed by a series of questions about why Meena needed help; how best to help; and what she had considered and discarded in her thinking.

After about 10 minutes Meena looked up. 'OK,' she said, 'I think I've got it and all you did is ask me a load of questions.' 'Ahh,' said Ashish, 'the answer was almost certainly in your head and you just needed help to get it out and into your document. The key thing was helping you to find the answers yourself.'

Meena may not have realised it, but by deploying a careful series of questions, Ashish had used a fundamental coaching technique to help her find her own solution to the problem she was facing.

Do this

→ **Find a model of coaching that works for you**
There are lots of books on coaching and your organisation may have a preferred model. Speak to your HR team and get their recommendation and help. If you are going to go solo, you might start with something like the widely used GROW (Goal, Reality, Options, Will/Wrap Up) model of Sir John Whitmore as a starting point.

→ **Learn the skills of questioning, listening and summarising**
Good coaching is essentially asking the other person questions to help them find a solution to their issue. Prepare a list of questions that work for you. Include the Who? What? How? When? Where? relating to the topic. Try to avoid using 'Why?' in this context as it can feel accusative.

Make sure you listen actively, signalling this so that the other person knows they are being heard. Give clear summaries to prove that you have heard what they said.

→ **Be comfortable with not having all the answers**
Suspend your personal need to have an answer to every question you ask. (This is difficult when your 'day job' is providing advice.) The art of coaching is to help the individual find their *own* solution to the issue at hand. Your job is to ask questions to help them think through that issue to find possible solutions – their own solutions.

→ **Practise, practise, practise**
Find people to practise on. Coaching is a skill and skills are only developed through practice. The more practice, the faster you will develop the skill and the better coach you will become.

→ **Get feedback**
Find a way to ask how you are doing too. Are you asking enough questions at the right time? Do you give clues that you are listening? Are you summarising at appropriate times? Use this information to improve your practice.

→ **Be clear in your mind: are you coaching for a 'skill' or a 'will' issue?**

Does the individual you're working with have the necessary skills to do the job? If not, show them how to do the task and explain why it is done in the way you are demonstrating. If the individual is unsure about the task, then you need to find out why.

→ **Develop range in your coaching style**

Coaching styles and techniques can differ widely, sometimes more directly enabling (providing a number of alternative ideas and asking the other person which they would chose, why, and how that might apply in their situation), sometimes more open-ended and non-directive. Experience and practice will help you determine when you should be more directive. As a general rule, start with the non-directive, open-ended style and only become more directive if the other person is really struggling.

→ **Encourage the other person to make the notes**

The actions from your coaching conversation are the responsibility of the person being coached. Encourage them to make notes. At a practical level, the act of writing down their actions becomes a subconscious commitment on the part of the writer. Put simply, they are more likely to follow through on their actions if they write them down.

→ **Realise that your teams may not know that you have been coaching them**

It is a truism that the better you become at coaching, the less obvious your skill is to the outsider – or those being coached. Do not expect all of your people to appreciate, and recognise, that you are developing their skills and knowledge. Some may simply be content to do exactly as they are asked.

→ **Grow your own coaches**

Select your best associates and teach them how to coach. Let them practise on you. Give them feedback and encourage them to coach their own juniors. Then check in with them to see how they are progressing. This will help build a culture of coaching in your business. Some of your people may need to be convinced of the value of coaching, others may actively encourage it because they understand its value or see it as a badge of executive status. While coaching is not a panacea for everything, it is a very effective way of developing others. Smart leaders need to be good at coaching themselves and to help their teams to learn this important skill too.

And remember

Used judiciously, coaching helps you grow the talent in your team. It supports positive and enabling workplace cultures and will help to build your reputation as a leader with everyone in the organisation.

While a 'one size fits all' coaching style touted as a panacea for every organisational ill is not appropriate, the smart leader knows that targeted and well-deployed coaching is an invaluable leadership tool, helping others to develop good judgement. We know it may take a bit longer to get the work done if you are teaching someone to find their own solutions rather than being more prescriptive. But one of your roles as a leader is to help your people to develop themselves by coaching them and helping them become coaches for their own people. The effort needed to do this is more than worthwhile; it builds self-reliance and can be used in many situations, including with clients.

Credibility

How much people believe and trust you is key to leading smart people – you need to be credible in their terms in their eyes. Early on, career credibility comes from technical expertise – but later in your career, this wanes unless one is truly an authority on a subject in a given domain.

At this later stage, credibility is directly related to track record and the responsibilities, projects or clients with which you are associated. Power and credibility are often inextricably linked to client or customer power. Credibility needs constant attention and reinforcement; it is an important source of power for leaders. The client–customer relationship leaders of the biggest, most prestigious and profitable clients tend to wield much more influence and power than others who manage smaller, less profitable/influential projects or clients. As a leader it follows that credibility is an important component of your ability to get things done.

Example

Xibao, an accountant by training, was a senior manager of a medium-sized 'niche' firm and running an average portfolio of clients, providing a wide breadth of general advice. He had one medium-sized national business that took up about 60 per cent of his available time along with a couple of smaller clients which, in effect, used up his spare capacity.

As he had some time available, he was asked to help a partner with another client that had a significant number of non-performing loans on its books. Xibao dived into the work, did it well and quickly gained a reputation as the 'go-to man' at the firm on non-performing loans. As he did more work on the topic, his expertise built and more work came his way. It led to him becoming a partner.

He accepted and pursued invitations to speak at events, to meet new prospective clients and other parts of the firm. He wrote articles for magazines and journals on the subject and his advice was sought after by industry bodies. Over the next 18 to 24 months he left behind his smaller clients and became fully deployed resolving non-performing loan issues, which was fast becoming a major growing line of business for the firm. His credibility in the topic became a self-reinforcing cycle based on his immersion in the work, while the fact that he was advising high-profile clients and driving business reinforced his position as a respected leader in his firm.

Do this

→ **Manage your current portfolio for maximum effect**
Ensure you hit your budgets – business development, utilisation, costs, billing and recovery targets – for your existing portfolio. This signals to others that you can be relied upon to deliver. That provides the currency to get you included on proposals and pitches for new work. It also demonstrates that you are able to manage a client account profitably.

→ **Be a business developer**
Either through your own efforts – or better still in conjunction with your colleagues – engage fully in your firm's priority business development activities. The stronger your client base, the better.

→ **Get yourself an 'edge'**
Build a reputation for something that is valuable to the firm. To build credibility you need to have an 'edge' – a reputation – something you are known for (for all the right reasons). Part of that may be your technical expertise. In most firms, very few partners are genuinely world class in a technical sense.

Instead, they derive their 'edge' from industry expertise, a contacts base, connections, or skill at handling 'awkward' clients.

→ **Don't underestimate your people skills**
Learn to run complicated, multidisciplinary projects or client teams for respected clients. Get some training to develop your interpersonal skills: the use of language, influence and persuasion, for example. Most organisations struggle to find enough people who can lead and manage people well, especially those who are really good at running complicated major projects or client accounts with multiple lines of business.

→ **Treat offers to join 'strategic' clients with caution**
Most firms have 'strategic' or trophy projects and programmes. Often these are big brand names that look attractive from the outside, something with which one would want to be associated. Indeed it may well be a sign of favour or prestige to be invited

to serve on XYZ Inc. because they are a Fortune 500 client. Consider such invitations carefully. There are times when such clients or programmes are difficult to make profitable and difficult to manage. While the work may not be technically cutting edge, the complexity of managing the account, the teams and the relationships can be hugely time-consuming. The upside is that such experiences may involve senior people in the organisation and provide good opportunities to expand networks and provide access to opinion-formers.

→ Treat everyone equitably

Credibility comes not just from how you handle your customers and clients. It is also derived from how you are perceived inside the firm. The way you treat your support staff, associates and peers also impacts your credibility.

→ Keep learning

Good leaders pay attention to their own development. They also go beyond the need for regulatory CPE. They are curious and learn from every experience with which they are presented. They view ongoing development as an opportunity to add to their knowledge and skills, modelling positive learning behaviours to team members too.

→ Be loyal

Repay loyalty to those who have contributed to the building of your reputation. No one likes to be abandoned. You may think that only one individual may be hurt or offended by disloyalty, but remember that others are watching. Their story of how you treated them will add to, or detract from, your credibility.

→ Be accountable

As a leader you have to make decisions and, sometimes, tough calls. How you do that, and how you own and stand by your decisions, will be keenly watched. When making tough calls, explain what you are doing and why; this all helps to get people 'on side' and build engagement.

And remember

For just about every leader today, maintaining or enhancing their personal credibility is an ongoing and vitally important task. You are only as good as your last project or assignment; so ensure that every project is as good as, or even better than, your last. For most leaders of smart people this means keeping up to date with a number of topics – and attempting to do so almost simultaneously.

The leader needs to be technically up to speed, knowing about the latest developments and where and how to access the relevant technical knowledge and information. In addition, s/he needs to stay abreast of what is happening in the organisation and among competitors. Leaders must also invest in personal and leadership skills. For the leader managing a smart team this should never be taken for granted. Your credibility needs continuous maintenance and personal investment.

Disruptors

It would be naïve in the extreme to expect any group of people to immediately agree, without question, with everything their leader might suggest. It is even more naïve when dealing with smart people. Professionals invariably have their own ideas about how things should be done. Often as not, they think they can do them better than anyone else and do not have a problem with making their views known. Even highly valued team members can express their views in a way that can have a destabilising effect. As group leader you need to determine whether the destabilising is positive or negative – both in intent and impact.

A smart leader's job is to provide the optimum amount of stability for the group, balancing high performance and innovation with managing conflict if debates or a clash of ideas or personalities threaten to disrupt in a negative way. At times this can be a tough balance to achieve. Remember: if you permit poor behaviour – you're promoting it.

Example

Rena closed the budgeting meeting, as usual, on time. As they left the room she asked 'What did you think, Dieter?' and an easy conversation followed about the flow of the meeting and the outcomes achieved. It was all a far cry from previous meetings. Dieter had a reputation with his colleagues as the person who would lob 'hand grenades' into the meetings, disrupting the flow of the discussion, being negative and continually restating his objections to proposed actions. Whilst Rena encouraged debate and discussion, Dieter's habitual objections were alienating him from his peers, his interjections eliciting eye-rolling and yawns from his colleagues.

The issue for Rena was that somewhere in Dieter's objections and negativity was invariably something worth hearing, an angle or risk that he alone seemed to be able to discern. In short, he potentially offered huge value; it just got lost in the awkwardness of his delivery. Over the last few months Rena had made extra efforts to speak with Dieter ahead of the meetings to get his views and to make space in the meetings for him to have specific input. She had provided Dieter with specific feedback on how he was impacting her (and by implication the rest of the team) and also how much she valued his insights. She coached him on how to make a bigger impact with his contribution.

Dieter had been aware that his input was not 'landing', but his frustration that others were not 'getting it' had unfortunately manifested itself in increasingly difficult behaviour. Over time Dieter cited his coaching and support from Rena as being instrumental in helping improve not only his performance in meetings but also his wider relationships and reputation in the company.

Do this

→ **Listen carefully**

No, really listen. What are the words saying to you? Remove any emotion you might be feeling and understand the words in the message. And then ask yourself, 'Why am I being told this now, by this person?' People always do things for reasons that make sense to them. You need to question both the message and the rationale before acting.

→ **Check the reality**

Consider whether you need to respond or react immediately; it might be better to wait. Take a long hard look at your own view of the situation. Are you overreacting? Is there a pattern of behaviour? Are you personally in a good place? Would you respond in the same way on a different day? Having 'grounded' yourself, decide when you need to take action.

→ **Identify if the effect is positive or not**

Encourage destabilising behaviour that you deem positive – even if it is poorly delivered. It will help your cause. For example, it may add weight

to an argument or situation that does not have the traction you desire with the group at large. Consider coaching and offer feedback if good ideas and intent are being poorly delivered.

→ **'Call out' mischievous behaviour**

Identify what you can do something about. Is it the words? The timing? The place of delivery? In these cases, speak quietly and privately with the individual. Explain what you saw and heard, the impact it had on you and what you observed to be its impact on the wider group. Ask the other person if this was their intention. If not, then help them learn how not to have the same impact again. Remember: how you deal with the individual concerned will be keenly watched – and analysed – by the rest of the group.

→ **Give feedback – when the effect is negative**

Go to the root cause. Listen to that person's point of view, offer feedback and tackle their motives and rationale. It may be worth having two (private) meetings, one to share the feedback and to ensure clarity of understanding, and a second to decide how to move forward. This might involve the use of sanctions.

In cases of repeated poor behaviour intended to make life difficult, your conversation needs to focus on *why* the individual is acting in such a manner. What are they trying to achieve? This may lead to a conversation about where the individual's interests might be best achieved in the longer term – and that might be in another organisation. Leadership is not a popularity contest, but it does require respect. If you cannot come to some mutual respect, then something has to change. Again, remember – everyone is watching.

→ **Be proportionate**

Act carefully and proportionately. Ask a trusted confidant(e) or two whether any sanction you are proposing seems reasonable. All people, but especially smart people, have a deep inbuilt sense of fairness. So make sure that any sanction you might use 'fits the crime'.

If the sanction is seen as too light then the severity of the misdemeanour gets lost. If it is too harsh people will stop trying

and talking with you, and your reputation will suffer. Smart people have long memories and will add the way you have handled difficult episodes to their version of your résumé that they carry in their heads.

→ **Clarify your expected standards of behaviour**

Make sure you have explained clearly what you expect, in behavioural terms, from your team. You want to encourage challenge, debate and creativity. But also, when decisions have been made, you want alignment and 'cabinet' responsibility with the execution. Explain and make it very clear how you want things to work. Always listen to suggestions, but sooner or later decisions need to be made and work needs to get done.

→ **Provide 'ways out'**

Always give the other person the benefit of the doubt – but with a limit. Give, allow or help the other person to find a 'face-saving' way out of a situation. Allow them to go back to their colleagues with their dignity and head held high, but not feeling patronised. Ask them how the resolution to the disagreement or issue can best be communicated for mutual benefit.

→ Consider ending it

As a last resort you may need to find ways of removing the person (or people). This is a step that should never be taken lightly – it is the use of naked organisational power, and the way you exercise your power sets a tone in your group.

Dismissal is always a last resort. It's better to enrol the support of someone who has hitherto been a destabiliser if at all possible. By doing this, you send out a powerful message about what good behaviour looks like and the importance of unity and everyone 'marching' together.

And remember

Dealing with destabilisers is something that needs sensitive handling and balance. You want to encourage creativity and innovation – but you also want the team to just get on and deliver the work.

Your reaction to these challenges becomes part of your reputation and how others experience themselves and you; it is a test of your values and what you believe. As a rule of thumb, remember: people don't need to lose for you to win. Aim to be firm, fair and friendly. But also accept that there is a time and place where a line will need to be drawn or you will lose respect and authority. And the importance of respect – especially when dealing with professionals – cannot be overstated. Lose respect and you have lost your leadership.

Decision-making

Decision-making is a key expectation everyone has of their leaders. And as a leader, the knowledge that the 'buck stops with you' on all manner of leadership, management and business challenges can be overwhelming. This is especially true for professionals who are used to relying on the certainty of what they know – their technical knowledge – as the basis for their decision-making. For technical professionals, it can be especially disconcerting to have to make decisions based on imperfect or partial information.

You may need to vary your style depending on the type of decision required, with whom it is taken, and for what reason. It may require persuasive reasoning, especially with smart technical people. Or you may need a set of steps to secure the commitment of others to a collective decision. If you are leading on a new initiative, your style may have to be visionary, starting with brainstorming and then honing down options.

Make sure you have involved or consulted the right people. This is not so that you can hide behind them; it's to access their wisdom and make sure you have considered all angles. Collaboration will also help formulate the narrative you need to explain your rationale for the decision. The crucial thing is knowing when to adopt a particular style, whether you really need 'hard technical information' or whether you should just be getting off the fence and getting a decision made.

Remember: there is no such thing as a perfect decision. One can only make the best possible decision with the information available at a moment in time. And recognise that we never have all the information we would like. It always is, at best, a judgement call, mitigated by the awareness and sensitivity to know when it might need changing in the future.

Example

Eguono and Ade had known each other since starting as graduate trainees at an international consulting firm. Now, many years later and still friends, they were also rivals, leading their respective firms. Eguono smiled as he put his mobile phone down. It was just like Ade to drop something out of 'left field'. He hadn't changed at all.

Ade had proposed a merger of their complementary geographic and sector specialist firms. To Eguono it was a 'no-brainer' decision. It just felt right – an opportunity for everyone in the firm. But was it the right decision? He thought back to a smaller acquisition they had made two years ago that had not gone well, even though that one had felt right at the time too.

This time it would be different. He decided he would involve as many people as possible in the decision-making process, especially those who would be most critical to implementation if the merger went ahead. Eguono realised that everyone knew he was Ade's friend, so a task force was going to be needed to ensure a balanced view.

Idaramfon was asked to bring her strong, independent questioning and robust challenges. She suggested co-opting one of their best associates; Ihuoma was universally respected for her technical knowledge and interpersonal skills. Serraj joined as the numbers person to drive the financial and market analyses. All brought different perspectives to the process and would be key to any successful implementation, acting as respected 'champions' in the firm.

One year later, Eguono reflected on the success of the merger. He realised his willingness to seek views and have his initial decision tested, build a team of differing perspectives, and involve those needed to implement any decision had made all the difference.

Do this

→ Select the core information you require

Take time to gather as much data as you can to inform your decision. If time is limited, prioritise the information-gathering by identifying which information will be most important. Sometimes you may have too much information, which if conflicting can result in *analysis paralysis*. Resolve this by setting a clear deadline for decision-making, including information-gathering.

→ Delegate the decision

Decide whether the decision is one you must make yourself, or can be made by one of your colleagues or associates who are closer to the issue. Could it be a good development opportunity? If appropriate, then delegate.

→ Decide how the decision is to be implemented.

Consider who will implement the decision. Does this affect who needs to be consulted as you take the decision? Make an initial assessment of who will be responsible for implementation and what authority and resources they might need.

→ Reflect on making the actual decision

Allow yourself time to reflect on the decision once it has been reached. Ideally, sleep on it before making an announcement. Once you are as certain as you can be with the current information, start communicating.

→ Be wary when using systematic techniques

Don't rely on computer-aided or artificial intelligence methods of decision-making. No automated technique can substitute for good judgement and clear thinking. Such techniques can provide useful data, a level of probability-sorting that is powerful and can inform the options available. But, in the end, all decision-making involves individual judgement. Systematic techniques are merely there to assist your own individual judgement, bravery, 'gut instinct' and commitment.

→ Consider the emotional as well as the rational

Get another view to balance your preferred bias. If you are a rational decision-maker (you prefer to rely on facts and data), get an emotional decision-maker (someone who is more at home with feelings, emotions and possibilities) to give you a perspective, and vice versa.

→ Recognise that you are probably dealing with dilemmas

Understand the nature of the decision you are making. Smart people are usually pretty good at making straightforward decisions on their own. This means that your leadership decisions will almost always involve dilemmas – where the choice is between two sub-optimal options – or tricky problems. Tricky problems – where there is contradictory or incomplete information, there are links to other issues, or because of the number of other people involved – will be fairly commonplace in professional, technical, scientific or other environments where smart people work. In these circumstances, consult widely to identify interdependencies and implications. Factor these into your selected solution(s) and monitor the ongoing situation to see how the decision is working out.

→ Not making a decision

Sometimes not making a decision is a decision in itself. However, make sure your inaction is done for good reason. It is not a licence for prevarication and delay.

And remember

Good decision-making requires investment in reflecting on decisions from the past, both good and bad, and especially bad. Essentially, having a post-mortem to consider the overall impact of the decision and how you made it: was it emotional, did you think through the consequences, did you select the route of least resistance?

Cognitively, we struggle to evaluate all the angles in a challenging situation, so bring in others for more diverse perspectives. But don't be afraid to act: make the decision and keep making progress with the team. And always remember: the worst decisions you make will probably be the decisions you make alone.

Delegating

Smart leaders have to make the time to delegate properly if they want a more effective team. Most professionals pride themselves on their ability to use their technical competence to solve problems or resolve issues and, as a result, tend to fix problems themselves. After all, fixing problems using one's professional experience is fun and interesting and makes use of hard-earned skills, talent and intelligence. However, what *leaders* need to do is delegate – especially when leading smart people.

Unfortunately, delegation is often deployed or done poorly. Usually this is down to time pressures, the perception that it's quicker to 'do it myself' or that everyone else is busy too. These may be valid concerns, but they don't take into account the fact that smart people need opportunities to stretch, grow and test themselves. Giving them these opportunities is critical to maintaining their work, engagement and enthusiasm. We know that the development of workplace skill, capability and judgement comes, in the main, from actually doing the work, reflecting on the experience, and where appropriate being supported by coaching and feedback. Delegation is a great way of providing developmental experiences on real work tasks.

Example

Ayesha was busy – in fact her whole team were busy. As a result, she tried to keep the team focused on their immediate deliverables while she personally absorbed the additional work that kept arriving. It was not long before a vicious circle started to 'bite' Ayesha. She was working flat out and struggling to keep her head above water and felt she did not have time to delegate properly. Then her team's staff satisfaction scores started to drop; they were bored doing the same stuff day in and day out, and rumblings about resignations started. This only added to the pressure Ayesha felt.

Concerned, Ayesha reflected, took advice from colleagues, and realised that she needed to change tack. Instead of taking on extra tasks herself, she used the time to delegate effectively. She cascaded as much work down to her team as possible. This was initially time-consuming – it would have been quicker in the short term to do the work herself – but she stuck to her guns and took the time to teach the team.

Before long, she was reaping the rewards. Her team of smart, ambitious people proved to be quick students, willing and able to take on new tasks, and open to new experiences. They appreciated that Ayesha had taken the time to delegate properly, outlining clearly her expectations for each task, and checking in with support, guidance and feedback where necessary. As well as spreading the workload, this focus on delegation built capability, confidence, work satisfaction, skill and loyalty among the team as a whole. Other people started to make approaches to join her team because of its reputation for interesting work opportunities. Investing time in delegation, while hard-won to start with, made Ayesha a better leader. She was no longer overwhelmed by a workload that got in the way of more actively managing her team and, at the same time, she had also given them opportunities to develop themselves and their own skills.

Do this

→ **Set clear parameters –
SMART+Q**
Be clear on the objectives of the
work that you are delegating.
Make sure the objectives
you agree with colleagues
are Specific, Measurable,
Achievable, Realistic and
have a Time-based element:
when you need the work done
by. Communicate clearly any
required qualitative standards,
such as customer feedback,
the content of conversations,
expected behaviour from
clients, how clients or
customers felt after receiving
the service.

→ **Agree your 'check-in' points in
advance**
Agree what and when you
will be checking in together.
Smart people don't really like
being checked up on. But they
generally are fine with it –
providing the check-in points
have been agreed in advance.
Schedule your follow-up
meetings. Do it now – and stick
to the schedule! No excuses.

→ **Explain the context**
Explain how the work fits into
the bigger picture. Explain
who it is for, what it is for, how
success will be measured.
Your colleagues are smart, and
clarity on these issues will allow
them to make decisions as they
progress.

→ **Check your colleagues'
motivation**
Ask them how they feel
about doing the work. Is this
something they have done
before? Are they confident?
Feeling like it is still a challenge?
If this is new to them, and they
are not feeling confident, they
will need more support. If it is
something they do not feel is
a challenge, then they need to
understand why you are asking
them to do it for a second or
third time.

→ **Assess your colleagues'
capabilities**
Check whether they have done
this sort of work before. Do they
have the skills to do the work;
if not, what skills, knowledge or
training might they need? How
will you help them acquire the
capabilities needed? Plan any

training jointly with them and recognise that a training course might not be the right answer. Time spent with you may be far more effective.

→ Check their understanding

Ask them to replay back to you their understanding of the work. They should do this in their own words. If they are simply repeating your words and phrases, challenge and ask them to explain it in their words. This step is an important check and will give you a clear idea of what you are likely to receive.

→ You can delegate responsibility, but *not* accountability

To execute the delegated task the individual must feel they are responsible for the work and getting it done. Ultimately, however, you are accountable, responsible for what happens on your watch. You will need to monitor and support, for example, providing the resources they'll need to deliver the task you have delegated to them. Delegation is about joint ownership, but accountability is the one thing that you cannot delegate.

→ Follow up

As soon as you have agreed the final plan with the team member, make sure you deliver on any commitments you might have made to help with information, resources, help, contacts. Their ability to deliver will be impacted by your failure to keep promises of support.

→ Recognise effort

Say 'thank you' and offer constructive feedback when the work is complete. Point out specifics that are good and positive. If there are things that could have been done better, share that in a way that helps them learn from the experience. Leaders forget how powerful a well-timed 'thank you' and other acknowledgements can be. They're a powerful tool in the smart leader's armoury.

→ Decide how specific you need to be when delegating

Decide how prescriptive you need to be for each of your team members or colleagues. This will depend on their previous experience of the work and the level of risk. Sometimes you need to be very specific in how you set objectives and at other times less so.

And remember

Delegating is never easy and smart leaders can always make up a thousand creative, credible and smart reasons to avoid delegating. The remedy is pretty straightforward. Get to grips with the idea that you are not helping yourself, your people or your organisation by hoarding work for yourself. You are probably creating stress for yourself and your team.

Sure, it may make *you* feel good and wanted to be busy. But the truth is that smart people want to develop and grow. The team may grumble about the extra work, but if they are learning by receiving challenging and stretching assignments, and also know that their leader is taking an interest in them, it will be appreciated and respected. Take the time and care effective delegation needs, including proper support, feedback and coaching. Smart leaders know that they get more back by giving away. They build a reputation for developing their people and teams and that is why other smart people want to be around them.

Empowerment and motivation

A fundamental issue in leadership is finding ways of aligning the effort of your followers in a way that requires minimal direction from you, the leader. How do you motivate smart, able people to deliver that extra effort? What can you do to motivate your followers to perform at their very best and give you the discretionary effort that is a clear indicator of a high-performing team?

Most professionals have a high need for achievement. This means they like to get things done, but often in their own way. They want to take charge of how they deliver the work; to take personal responsibility for it; to be challenged (*note*: challenged – not overwhelmed); to be autonomous; to set high standards for themselves – in short, to be the very best that they can be. They are motivated by challenging, tough, intellectually demanding problems and questions.

The reality is that it is more or less impossible to motivate another person, but you can create an environment and the circumstances in which they feel empowered and want to give their absolute best. It's all about the right balance of challenge and support.

Example

A young associate, Vijay, was sent by a client partner to an emerging market for an extended period to lead on a transaction for an established and valued client of the firm. The client had got itself into major difficulties in a country where it was out of its depth. The work in itself was challenging, at the very edge of Vijay's competence and experience.

Vijay was smart and ambitious, motivated by just these kinds of challenging opportunities. But he was also aware of how much was riding on the assignment, for his own and his firm's reputation. It was not going to be easy, especially so far away from his home base. As he flew in and took stock of the situation, he could see that he might be overwhelmed by the expectations placed upon him.

However, Vijay's fears were unfounded, largely because of the right support from David, the partner. David called every day. His calls were always about 'us' and whether 'we' were OK. Did we need extra resources from headquarters? Was there anything further he could do to help? If a resource or support was required, he delivered. He even made sure Vijay's personal life was going well.

By providing this kind of care and support, David created the right environment for Vijay to succeed. He knew that Vijay's natural motivation to do a good job would only be enhanced by giving him the practical tools and emotional confidence to help him perform to the best of his abilities.

Do this

→ **Pay attention to the working 'climate' you are creating**
Make sure work is challenging and of the right quality for your team. Clear yourself out of the way, but be there to help and support. Make sure they have the tools to do the job. Provide feedback regularly. Coach, challenge and involve your people in setting their performance targets.

→ **'Know' your people**
Recognise that most of your team members will have a high need for achievement. Because the intrinsic challenge in doing the work is really important to them, the nature of the work they do is really important. If they get bored, they will find a new role or employer, someone who will allow them to exercise their intellect and problem-solving skills.

→ **Review the work coming in ... regularly**
In an ideal world you would decide which work was worthy of your team and refuse or disengage from unprofitable, technically unchallenging work that did not fit with the practice profile you were trying to build. In the real world, where we have to deal with revenue or sales targets, this is not always possible.

Make every effort to supply your people with interesting and challenging assignments that will help them learn and grow their skills and capabilities. If you do have to get a lot of routine work done, try and find ways of allowing them to be creative in either the scope of the work or the manner of delivery. If neither are possible, then make sure you explain why the tasks need to be done and when interesting tasks or opportunities will likely be available. Smart people hate being bored.

And do make sure your people know why seemingly poor-quality work is being accepted and needs to be done. It will help them make sense of the seeming inconsistency.

→ **Don't just focus on money**
Make sure your financial compensation and benefit arrangements are within the market range for comparable jobs elsewhere. But in jobs that

require creativity, talent and the application of knowledge, money is not always the prime motivator. This is not the same as saying money is unimportant because money is often used by professionals as a proxy for their importance and how well they are regarded in the organisation. Your overall compensation and benefits need to facilitate your people's need for recognition and status among their peers.

→ **Stretch and challenge your team – all the time**
See every job or task as a potential motivator for team members. Wherever possible, push work down to the most junior member of your team

capable of doing the work. Delegate properly, then help them deliver it and provide ongoing feedback.

→ **Show them the big picture**
Make sure your people know where they fit into the strategy for the growth and development of the business. They need to know how their contribution fits into and leads towards the end goal.

→ **Create recognition rituals**
Start team meetings with recognising someone from the team who has gone above and beyond for a client or the firm. You are accountable for your followers' recognition.

And remember

You can only motivate your people by creating the systems and environment that makes them want to do their very best. Their motivation is intrinsically inside them. Your job as the leader is to create an environment that is super-attractive to your smart, intelligent, able people. A place where they feel psychologically safe and able to deliver of their very best for you. A place where they know they can safely stretch themselves because, even if they do fall short, they will still be supported and their efforts recognised.

Leaders who are able to empower their teams create huge value across the organisation. Accessing such discretionary effort, freely given, becomes contagious. The trick is to create a truly empowering work environment where challenge and support work hand in hand to amplify the effort of the individuals.

Feedback/ feed-forward

Letting smart people know how they are doing can be challenging. Self-consciously high achievers invariably have high aspirations and can be reluctant to accept or take on board constructive feedback. But giving these people developmental feedback in a way that leads to positive outcomes is a core leadership skill that must be mastered. It's crucial for building individual capability in team members and, therefore, the organisation as a whole. Feedback needs to be neutral in delivery yet powerful enough to encourage change. It needs to be specific, timely and well judged. Fortunately, as with other leadership skills, it can be learnt and developed with practice.

Being able to deliver feedback is only one part of the job. Feedback, inevitably, is based on the past and what has happened. Sometimes it is more helpful to the individual to receive 'feed-forward'. This means offering timely suggestions, thoughts or ideas for how to improve or move forward. This can, of course, be part of a coaching conversation or simply some pointers to help someone get started when they are unsure. Consider the best way to engage with the smart individual; does that person respond better to clear direction or a nudge to help them work it out for themselves?

Example

Steve was delighted with the presentation Charlotte, a junior member of his team, had delivered at the divisional board meeting. It had just the right amount of detail, some nice touches of humour, and great structure. The summary at the end had been masterful. Steve felt certain the board had been given all the facts on which to base their decision.

Steve caught up with Charlotte later that day and shared the feedback that, overall, the board had found the work outstanding. He cited several specifics from the presentation, leaving her in no doubt about how good a job she had done.

However, Steve also realised that he could use the feedback session to help Charlotte improve even further. He asked Charlotte to recall one of the more testing questions she had received at the presentation and how she thought that she had answered it. She candidly said that she thought her reply was weak and perfunctory. He went on to ask how she might have answered it differently. After a couple of minutes' thought, Charlotte confessed to not having a clue. Steve did not push her for an answer. Instead, he shared with her three tips, based on his experience, of things that had worked for him, with specific examples.

He offered clear ideas, presented as options, of things Charlotte might consider trying (in her own style) next time around. Charlotte listened and easily picked up on the ideas as they were relevant to her area of work. She started to combine elements of Steve's ideas into her next presentations. It would have been easy for Steve just to say 'Good job' to Charlotte and move on. However, he chose to be a smart leader and feed-forward too, by identifying an area where Charlotte could improve and giving her the tools to help her visualise exactly what that improvement might look like.

Do this

→ **Check your mindset**
Ask yourself: what purpose will this feedback serve? What is your intention? If it is not positive and focused on development, and the issue isn't urgent or serious, wait and find another time or way of doing it. Good intention on your part is paramount.

→ **Be clear on the message**
Construct your message carefully. And keep it short and to the point. The message needs to be clear, precise and succinct.

→ **Pick your moment**
Choose your moment carefully. Are they ready to hear this message now? Is this a good time for them? If they are in the middle of a crisis or having issues at home, it may not be a good time. This is not simply a humane consideration. They simply won't hear the message if they are preoccupied with something that to them is more important.

→ **Make sure you have the data**
Be very clear and cite specific examples of the behaviour you experienced. Without examples your feedback is meaningless. Examples help the other person reflect upon their behaviour in a meaningful, contextualised way.

→ **Choose your words and tone carefully**
Be brief and very clear – make sure there is no accusatory tone in your voice or implication in your words.

→ **Select the right time and place**
Choose a right time and place for the conversation. If it is a positive message, then in public may well be good. If the feedback is negative or constructive, then it must be delivered in private, and one-to-one. Pay attention to your surroundings. Are they conveying messages of status and hierarchy that you are not aware of? Is there a physical barrier like a table between you?

→ **Use a formula that works for you**
Start by raising the topic, and check – is now a good time to talk about this? (If not – then when?) 'I'd like to talk about X … can you recall the experience?' Ask them to replay it from their

perspective. Then offer the feedback – what was good, what impact it had. Ask if that was the impact they were intending. Share the feedback, with data, about the impact. Ask them for a reaction. Then ask how they might do it differently next time. If they are struggling, offer ideas and suggestions.

→ **Choose when to feed-forward**
Feed-forward simply means to offer ideas and suggestions for help when someone is struggling. The key issue is choosing the 'right' time to offer the advice. Too early and

the other person may not learn or develop; too late and the moment may have gone. There is no hard-and-fast rule for this other than intuition and experience, also asking the other person if they have any ideas themselves.

→ **Look out for changes**
Keep an eye out for the person and when they are handling similar situations or circumstances in the future. Make sure you praise them and reinforce any positive changes they exhibit.

And remember

We firmly believe that the vast majority of people come to work with the intention of doing a good job and not making life difficult for their colleagues. As such, receiving constructive or negative feedback may be more of a shock than one might realise. We really like the idea of feed-forward: helping people figure out what to do differently by offering them clues, a nudge or some advice based on your experience of their work.

Formal or planned feedback is often associated with negative or constructive messages. However, don't overlook the power of giving proper feedback when people are doing well. Consider, too, how to use feed-forward to build on positive performance or behaviours with ideas for doing ever better.

Ignore any misplaced advice to use the good news/bad news/good news 'sandwich' format for feedback. It is horrible, obvious and especially irritating to smart people. Our 'formula' is to begin with good intention; raise the topic, supported by data; get a reaction and rationale; seek alternatives; and then discuss what could be done next time.

It takes many more instances of positive feedback to compensate for a negative comment – especially one that is delivered badly. So, observe your people doing good stuff and tell them whenever you can. It helps them understand that they are doing OK. It's also good leadership.

Giving praise

Smart leaders support their people to grow and develop into self-sufficient leaders in their own right. To grow skill and capability, people need to understand what they need to do, and, most importantly, when they have done things 'right'. This means giving praise and positive feedback.

When we are in a hurry, finding time to give praise that confirms people are 'on the right track' can get lost in the hurry and busyness of the day. Smart people often have well-honed critical faculties that focus easily and quickly on identifying problems rather than thinking of opportunities to praise. The leader of smart people knows that the key thing is to catch people doing things well and make sure that the person knows that they have been seen doing good stuff. Help your people really understand what 'good' looks like.

Example

An executive team was very worried about a culture of negativity in their business. The firm employed a lot of very bright, really smart people. They were also really good at finding fault with each other and at sharing their feedback vocally. It had created a cycle of negativity in the business that was starting to grow. It was also beginning to have an adverse effect on business performance.

The executive team knew they had to act. As part of a set of remedial measures, they agreed that every day each of them would 'Catch Someone Doing Something Right' and then tell them, in public if at all possible. Irrespective of who it was, they made a point every day of commenting positively on something specific they had seen or heard from people in the offices. And they held each other to account on a regular basis.

Over time, this idea caught on as other leaders were coached to emulate the example set by the executive team. More importantly the mood in the organisation brightened and levels of engagement, as measured in the annual people surveys, improved markedly.

Do this

→ **Catch people doing stuff right – and tell them**

As you walk around, observe your colleagues doing good things and tell them. Give them the specifics and let others see that you have recognised good work.

→ **Be specific**

Be specific about positive behaviours and actions. For example, 'That was a great meeting you ran, Anil' doesn't tell Anil what he needs to do to run another good meeting. Instead say, 'The way you kept summarising at regular intervals made that meeting really effective.' That is information Anil can use in the next meeting. Telling people they have been a big help is nice, but not always a lot of use.

→ **Be balanced**

Remember the ratio: five pieces of good/positive feedback or praise are needed in order to compensate for one piece of harsh or negative feedback. Recognise the impact you are likely to have in delivering critical feedback and create an appropriate balance.

→ **Don't overdo it**

Finding a balance in the amount of praise you give is important. Overdoing it can devalue its currency. It also makes others question your motives and sincerity. By the same token, scarcity does *not* make praise more valuable.

→ **Make it a habit**

Set yourself a target for each week to catch a few people and to tell them. Catch your peers, your boss, your people and other leaders' people. Don't discriminate across the hierarchy; it is equally important for you as a leader to recognise the most junior person in the office and the most senior. Pretty soon you'll get a reputation as a great leader who really helps develop other people. That's worth a huge amount.

→ **Make it physical and personal**

Make your praise visible. Try keeping a stock of compliments slips, post-it notes (jokey ones if you like) or postcards. When you catch someone doing something cool, good or neat, write them a card or note and leave it on their desk, computer or workstation. Use team meetings or calls to acknowledge contributions. But be specific: who did what and when.

→ **Find a specific formula – a form of words that work for you**
When telling people what they have done right, make it crystal-clear. Use a formula that looks something like this: when it happened, what you saw or heard, and the impact it had on you – or that you saw in others. The acid test is whether, after you have told them, they are able to do something with the information.

→ **Don't let people diminish it**
Often, when receiving praise people will say, 'Oh it was nothing' or something similar. Don't let it go. Tell them, in your words, that it did not seem so to you; that you really appreciated it and why. Don't let them off the hook.

And remember

One of the reasons we don't give praise – or positive feedback – as often as we should is that it can feel awkward to do so, as does receiving it. And to make things worse, it feels awkward to watch the recipient feeling awkward. We just don't know what to say when someone says nice things to us.

Smart leaders do know and help people to receive praise too. The simplest way of responding to praise is to say a simple 'thank you' and leave it at that. Teaching others this simple trick encourages positivity across teams and organisations.

Impact and presence

To be taken seriously as a leader you need to look, act and sound like one – and not only with your direct reports, but also with your colleagues, clients and stakeholders. We are not advocating some sort of stereotypical, heroic, 'alpha' behaviour pattern; we're talking about leaders – whether they are larger than life or more subdued and quiet – who express a degree of confidence and calmness.

Leaders with coherent personal impact and presence make a strong impression which is a big help in getting things done. They embody confidence and clear communication, which inspires and creates trust and engagement. They know that first impressions are formed very quickly – often in the first 10 seconds and then confirmed over the next five minutes. An air of realistic, authentic confidence is contagious. Smart people expect their leaders to have confidence in what they are doing and where they are leading.

Example

Anil was the senior partner of a firm that had announced that it was to merge with a competitor. This was great news for the firm and Anil's group in particular. Yet, everyone was worried about redundancies. Anil was expert in his area of technical specialisation but uncomfortable when speaking to a group of over three people. A 'town hall' meeting of the entire department's 120 staff was called.

Anil knew public speaking was not his forte and that he needed help. In conversation with his mentor, he realised he needed to provide reassurance for his colleagues and to help keep up morale and sustain business continuity. His mentor also helped him to understand that he might never be a natural public speaker, but that he could find his own way to create the confidence his group needed to see from him.

To ensure he got his message across, Anil scripted the salient points, crafting it so that it was as brief as possible and he got the words exactly right. He took steps to mentally prepare himself for the presentation so as to leave the group with a positive feeling while also being realistic about the changes they faced.

On the day of the meeting he arrived early and had conversations with a number of his colleagues to break the ice, and to judge the atmosphere and make himself more comfortable. When the time came, he remembered his mentor's advice to take deep breaths, stand tall, and make eye contact. He explained clearly that he was going to use his script to make sure he covered everything – and then read from his notes. Afterwards he took questions – a format he found much more comfortable – and circulated around the room, joining small groups to address questions and concerns.

Afterwards, his colleagues commented on Anil delivering the message 'true to his style' and not trying to do or be something he was not. They were reassured by his confidence in making the presentation in his own style, combining the necessary 'town hall'-style overview with communication in smaller groups. Anil had rightly judged that he needed to step up as the group's leader, but found a way to do so that was authentic and sincere.

Do this

→ **Be clear about the impact you want to have**

Start with the end in mind. What impact do you want to make and what will that look, sound and feel like? How do you want others to experience you? Get feedback on your self-image, projected image and received image. Ask your trusted confidant(e)s.

→ **Posture**

Face people directly when you're talking to them. A quarter-turn away signals a lack of interest and can make the other person feel you are distracted and not interested. Making a positive impact with your physical presence suggests ease with yourself and what you are saying. Impactful leaders adopt a variety of styles – but they always seem relaxed and 'comfortable in their own skin' which conveys inner confidence.

→ **Eye contact**

Scan your audience and make eye contact with the majority of them, even if momentarily. When shaking hands, have a steady gaze. When making a point, use direct eye contact to create emphasis. We use eye contact as a proxy for honesty and commitment. One proviso: beware cultural differences.

→ **Use your voice**

Put as much energy as you can into your voice by breathing fully and deeply.

This will make your voice more powerful, compelling and authoritative. Commanding a room when speaking helps with buy-in and commitment. Hesitation such as 'ers' and 'ums' can suggest uncertainty or discomfort. You need to speak in your own way with as much confidence, certainty and conviction as you can muster.

→ **Be authentic**

'Walk the talk' of your personal values and the values of the organisation. If you pretend to be something you are not, people will see that and remember the inconsistency. Consider your strengths, your values, how you want to be. Are these visible in the way you speak and behave?

→ **Be aware of your body language**

Remember: people will be influenced by the non-verbal elements of your communication – your body language – as well as voice. What you say is enhanced or diminished by your body language. People pick up clues about how much caring, warmth, inclusion and openness they detect in your behaviour. Warm body language is about positive eye contact, smiling and open body postures.

→ **Mirroring and matching**

Be aware of your own behaviour and use it to enhance your connection with others. We automatically begin to match the stance, arm and hand positions, facial expressions, voice and energy of people we like or agree with. We seem to pick up these signals when we are connected and engaged, so consciously being aware of, and managing, our own behaviour can make our communication easier and more powerful.

And remember

Creating and maintaining positive impact and presence requires work, but is important for smart leaders. After all, who wants to work with someone who doesn't seem to have any enthusiasm and presence? It begs the question of how well such a leader is able to represent and champion the interests of their people. Leaders have a huge variety of styles and skills that they deploy, but instilling confidence in their teams is particularly important for teams made up of smart people.

The bottom line here is to always have in mind how you are being seen and experienced by the team. Try and exert as much control as you can by being mentally prepared for any situation: what might be the concerns or inner distractions you have to overcome? Reflect on the impact of your physical presence and voice. Where is there room for improvement? Find ways to positively enhance your posture and voice, as well as the words you use. Adapt your style to your environment, the tone and the mood of the situation. And remember: smart, discerning people are looking for authenticity. You need to find techniques that help you to create your own maximum impact and presence.

Having necessary conversations

One of the hallmarks of a good leader is their ability to give clear and unambiguous messages. Partly, this means giving cues as to what is right and appropriate behaviour and what is not. One of the few tools you have with very smart people is your ability to communicate clearly, using every means available to encourage aligned behaviour.

Communicating clearly will, at some stage, inevitably involve the delivery of bad news: a promotion denied; a colleague who is not performing; making someone redundant. These are all conversations that as leaders we may not relish (and may avoid through delay and diversionary tactics) and hope will go away. They always do. The curious thing is that the old adage from tax lore applies equally to these circumstances: pay now or pay later with interest. This translates to: have the honest conversation now, even if it is difficult, or do it later when it has, in all probability, become even more awkward.

Example

Peter was a well-known client partner, respected and liked throughout his firm and popular with his team. Younger colleagues were keen to work with him and quite rightly; they had much to learn from his technical expertise and his skill in managing clients.

Peter also had high expectations of his team, who themselves had developed a reputation for high performance and total commitment. But one new member of the group was causing Peter concern. Max had joined from another company and seemed to be struggling with the step up that a relatively early promotion meant for him. He wasn't making the progress he should. Peter knew that things weren't working out, but hoped that Max's undoubted intelligence would see him through.

Max was himself aware that things were not going well. At the end of his probation period, he asked Peter directly about his performance. On the back foot, Peter failed to take the opportunity to vocalise his concerns about Max's performance and instead made some non-specific and non-committal comments that it was early days yet and he was sure that things would get better.

They didn't. Max was clearly out of his depth and continued to struggle. His colleagues began to resent the fact that he was not able to pull his weight. In the end, Peter had to face the fact that he would have to let Max go – a process that was much more difficult and stressful for both parties given that Max had been confirmed in his position and had not been given honest feedback about how he was progressing. By avoiding an honest conversation at the right time, Peter had done himself and Max no favours.

Do this

→ **Don't avoid the conversation**
Recognise when such conversations are needed and be proactive in planning for and holding the conversation in good time. These conversations are important 'statements' about what is important to you as leader. Leaving them – or worse, avoiding them – simply makes them even more difficult and potentially less impactful when they do come to pass.

→ **Start with good intentions – your mindset is crucial**
Change your mindset: this is simply a normal conversation where there may be different points of view. Above all keep focused on achieving a positive outcome. This is a conversation between two smart grown-ups who need to come to a joint agreement about how to move forward on an issue. It is nothing more or less.

→ **Listen – really listen**
Listen deeply and show you are listening to their version of the story. Take time to process the other person's tone, words and body language. Use silence to give people time to absorb what you have said. Give them time to think and respond. Above all don't feel the need to fill the silence, the pauses. Leading smart people means always winning the head as well as the heart – and usually in that order. Key to winning both is to ensure that the other person knows they have been heard.

→ **Prepare but don't script**
Know how to begin – 'I would like to talk with you about what happened with x client and why we missed the deadline.' Do your homework, for example, how their behaviour negatively affected the team/business. Keep your language simple, clear and emotion-free. And don't use hearsay and gossip. Smart people have a keen ear for discrepancy and contradiction. Be able to recount your own evidence to support your case if needed. Don't assume that your version is shared with the other person. Be open to different potential routes: do not go in with a start and an end and nothing in between.

→ Know your objective

Be very clear, in your mind, of the purpose of the conversation. Most importantly, what do you want the other party to actually *do* as a result of the conversation? Is it a change in future behaviour or something that should be done now? Be very clear on the 'ask' you have as a result of the conversation.

→ Pick the time and place with care

Remember it is important where you have the conversation. Bear in mind what messages the location may convey. A bar or restaurant may belie any seriousness. An office (your own or borrowed) will convey (even if only subconsciously) messages of power, status and hierarchy. And bear in mind what the timing will convey either to add or diminish the seriousness. Over breakfast or lunch may mean it is just something to be fitted in. A long formal appointment may send a message out of all proportion to the seriousness of the conversation.

→ Don't let your emotions take over

Control any frustration and anger you might feel. Equally, have the emotional

sensitivity to show empathy and understanding. Recognise and acknowledge the other's emotion. Refer to it – 'I can hear you feel very strongly about this' – but don't criticise, diminish or dismiss their emotion. Human behaviour is driven, in the main, by emotions and it will have driven the other person's behaviour. You ignore this at your peril.

→ Manage the conversation

Slow the pace, keep the tension down and give your full undivided attention. Put your smartphone away. Give the other person plenty of opportunity to speak. They need to have the chance to respond.

→ Keep it simple

Be clear on your message and deliver it succinctly. Give bad news upfront and don't 'sugarcoat' it with unrelated matters. Above all don't patronise the smart people with whom you are working – it is a surefire way of irritating them.

→ Help others to reach the end point

Keep your desired end point in mind. The route to getting there is less important. You have a reason for choosing to have the conversation with the other party. If you seek their commitment to make some changes, then be authentic, respectful and don't ambush them. Help them find a way out – to save face – that demonstrates that you respect them as a person. For smart people, that respect for them and their ideas is important. As the leader it also signals to others how you deal with such issues.

→ **Check if there is a 'third story'**
Often in difficult conversation around conflict there is your story and your counterpart's story. There is mileage in searching for the third 'real story'. It can be about perceptions.

→ **Re-label the conversation!**
Don't call these conversations 'bad news' or 'difficult'. The very nomenclature you use will affect how you view and approach the conversations. One easy step is to simply label them in your head as important conversations that need due care and attention. View them as 'important', 'honest', 'straight-talking' – in fact anything that helps you deal with it in a positive frame of mind!

And remember

Yes, these conversations often are difficult and you should not try and disguise that. Difficult conversations are difficult not just because we have to face the other person, but also because we have to face ourselves. What is important is how you handle them.

When you are leading smart people, having difficult conversations is inevitable and your people expect you to handle these conversations well. We make these conversations harder, though, by labelling them as 'difficult'. So, do yourself a favour and inject a degree of realism into your own internal dialogues. Do not frame them as difficult conversations, but rather as 'straight-talking' or honest conversations, or however you choose to label them. But stop referring to them as difficult – or the difficulty will be magnified in your own mind. Remember: putting off an honest conversation can have dire consequences; the issue won't go away, and the time that has elapsed is only likely to exacerbate it. You don't have to enjoy having these conversations, but you do need to be good at having them.

Resolving conflict

Smart people tend to have opinions. Often deeply held ones. As a result, not everyone is going to agree with you all of the time. In a real team of diverse smart people, that likelihood is even higher.

The paradox is that conflict can be one of the forces that, managed carefully, will drive extraordinary levels of performance. For others, conflict is awkward and something to be avoided at all costs. Navigating this potential minefield is the responsibility of the leader. You will experience conflict with and between team members. And you will need to manage it. The ultimate goal is to harness the passion and energy conflict generates and direct it towards achieving great results for the group.

Example

Mario was relieved to return to the calm of his own office. Yet another team meeting had spiralled out of control, with two of his best performing people, Mark and Ellie, clashing over even the smallest point of difference. Both were smart and ambitious, but also had very different approaches to their work. Mark was conscientious and preferred to work collaboratively. He seemed to resent what he perceived to be Ellie's more aggressive and direct style. They were stuck in a pattern of behaviour that was beginning to impact negatively on their work, and on the team.

It was time for Mario to act. He needed Mark and Ellie to recognise that their behaviour was unacceptable, while also helping them to respect each other's ways of working. After meeting with each of them individually, clearly spelling out the problem and listening carefully to their frustrations, he realised that they had much more in common than they might have thought. Both were passionate about their work and shared the goal of making their team the best in the industry.

When the next big project came up, Mario invited Mark and Ellie into his office. He suggested that they had the complementary skills and approaches to make the project a success and asked them to work together on its implementation. Despite some initial consternation, Mark and Ellie were able to find common ground in their determination to make the project work. Sparks still flew from time to time, but Mario had been smart in finding a forum which forced them to acknowledge each other's strengths and to work together towards an overarching goal.

Do this

→ **Take responsibility**
As leader, you are responsible for resolving conflicts. This doesn't mean that you have to do all of the work yourself, but you will need to find the forums, words and combinations of people to enable the conflict to be worked through. It may require several conversations to reach lasting agreement.

→ **Surface it**
People feel when there is conflict. So call it out. Give it names or labels. Simply saying 'We seem to have a serious difference of view here' focuses attention. And note the use of the word 'seem'. It appears simple enough but this also signals that you may have partial understanding. Surfacing the issues is an essential skill. If you do not, the issue will resurface of its own accord somewhere, sometime. And usually it will be an inconvenient time.

→ **Listen first**
Suspend your immediate reaction. Start by listening – really hard. Listen, repackage and replay what you think you have heard. Test it. Did you get it right? Has it altered your perspective?

→ **Depersonalise your language**
Use words like 'we' as opposed to 'you'; 'What alternatives do we have?' versus 'Have you thought of anything else?' Your aim is to keep the individual from feeling attacked or that they are the only person being held responsible.

→ **Don't die in a ditch unnecessarily**
Remind yourself that your job as the leader is to play the long game. Is the current battle really going to cost you the war or do you have room to manoeuvre?

→ **Be magnanimous**
Ensure both parties are able to retain their dignity. Be magnanimous but not patronising. Others do not have to lose for you to win. No one likes losing and everyone dislikes being reminded that they have lost. If it is a particularly big or public issue, ask the other side how best you can communicate the resolution so that 'face' is saved on both sides.

→ Stop it becoming personal

Focus on the issue or the topic. Do not attribute it or link it directly to individuals. For example, 'If we talk about raising prices' is very different from 'Your argument for raising prices'. If you say 'your', you will almost certainly elicit a defensive reaction from the other party. Keep the issue separate from the individual.

→ Come to a conclusion

Be clear on next steps. People hate being stuck. Finding next steps, or points or actions to move towards, is key to a resolution. Even a partial step forward is better than no step forward at all. Find areas where people can agree. Link them together and co-create a way forward that is acceptable to both of you. You can accept and commit to the solution even if it is less than you actually wanted if it shows progress.

→ Retain the relationship

Thank the aggressor for raising and debating the issue that resulted in the conflict, the tenacity with which they have debated it or represented their stakeholders. You want them to feel committed to the solution and, equally importantly, for them to feel that they are able to come back and raise other issues. Who knows? Those issues may be even more 'mission-critical' than the topic they had raised originally.

→ Expect a degree of personality-driven conflict

Smart people will disagree with each other. The job of the leader is to get clarity. Why is there conflict? If it is about means, methods, objectives or tangible things, these can be discussed and ways forward agreed. If it is simply personal animus then there is a need, at the right time, to talk about it – either one-to-one or possibly in the group. It may mean that working practices need to be reworked, or new protocols developed. In the most extreme of cases, it may mean one or both parties need to move on and leave the group. Although this may be difficult, the leader needs to bear in mind the needs of the team as a whole.

→ Find the third story

Be clear on your story – what is your version of the events or issues? Write it down. Now write down the other party's version – their story. Test it – have you got it right? Now, with the other side, figure out the third story – the combined one that builds on successes and areas of commonality. The one that makes progress. Do you both agree to it?

And remember

Sometimes harmony is just not possible. But beware of 'agreeing to disagree'. You are leading smart people. That means they are skilled in the use of language and, more importantly, their interpretation and construction of what the words used really mean. The expression 'wriggle room' could almost have been invented to describe how smart people get themselves out of commitments with which they do not feel happy. Your skill as a leader is to get everyone to agree to a course of action that makes progress towards an overall goal – without reducing everything to a suboptimal lowest common denominator.

Above all think about what consensus really means. In our world, reaching consensus means you can broadly agree with something such that action can be taken. It means that you agree with it and will defend the decision. It means that you have argued your point but have come to agreement that other views must prevail and, for the common good, you have accepted an agreement for the good of the group. Sometimes, even smart people need to be reminded of this.

Setting objectives

Smart leaders are clear about desired results. They outline goals and objectives in such a way that puts their people's smart technical knowledge into a clear manageable perspective. This provides a route map for individuals to progress and an effective means of managing performance.

However, setting and monitoring objectives is not always straightforward, especially in an era of remote and flexible working practices. Knowledge work does not always lend itself to more quantitative goals and setting objectives for things that are not easily measurable can be difficult. The key is making sure that all the main task parameters are clearly understood, providing support and agreeing relevant check-in or review points.

The much-used and simple mnemonic SMART+Q is a good starting point when setting and agreeing objectives that are clear and have the intended effect – to create the building blocks that contribute to team and company goals and strategies. 'Agreeing' is also an important word here. Objectives are much more likely to be met if the person tasked with achieving them is involved in framing them in the first place.

S stands for Specific, M for Measurable, A for Achievable, R for Realistic and T for Timed.

Specifics are things like delivery time, time needed for the job, cost, expenses, nature of the final work product.

Measurable means allocating sensible numbers or standards for the work.

Achievable is a simple check that this task is able to be completed: can it be done?

Realistic: ask whether the work can be done within the agreed parameters with the available resources.

Timed: what are the staging/time phases for the piece of work – including reviews?

The +Q is a reminder to include the necessary qualitative measures. For instance, are there specific individuals who need to be consulted/involved? Does the work output need to be formatted using the clients' branding? How do they want it delivered? The qualitative metrics are nearly always harder to work out, but are essential for people working in knowledge-based industries where simple metrics do not tell the whole story. This is especially important when the work involves client interactions.

Example

Fatima was reviewing the Statement of Work from the leader of the project office. It was very clear – in broad terms – what she needed to achieve; what she needed to do was to decide how she wanted to deliver the project in practice.

The time deadline for the first phase of the project was exactly 90 days which, though achievable, would be a stretch. Specifically, it would likely need 120 hours of time to prototype, build and test the process within the workshop. Crucially, the process needed to be able to replace the current system at the end of the testing period – that piece was clear.

The next thing to consider was who had the necessary skill and experience to do the job. That was relatively straightforward too; she had already discussed the project with a team who had done this kind of work before and would not be fazed by the tight deadline. They had contributed some really good ideas for how implementation could be improved.

It was then that she remembered the requirement in the contract that stipulated certain operating protocols (including qualitative customer feedback) to which they needed to adhere. Failure to do so would incur financial penalties. She added these requirements to her growing list. Sitting back, with her pad in front of her, Fatima checked off her notes. This certainly looked SMART+Q.

By using the SMART+Q framework, Fatima had been able to marshal her thoughts and to break down the larger goal of project delivery into its constituent parts. Setting her own high-level objectives also helped, in turn, to agree SMART+Q objectives with the people who would support the project's implementation.

Do this

→ **Be very clear on *all* aspects of the deliverables**
Be clear on both the quantitative and qualitative aspects of the task. What are the key elements that need attention and by which success will be measured? Write these down and make sure they are agreed.

→ **Use the mnemonic SMART+Q**
Work with your team members to secure their ideas and input as to what metrics are appropriate and sensible for the work in hand. Ask them what they think is realistic. Use your experience to make a judgement, then think about others' knowledge, experience and motivation around the task and use those thoughts to come to an agreement. As a rule of thumb always get a view from others first. Remember, for professionals and knowledge workers it is important for their motivation for them to feel that they have some control over their task parameters.

→ **Make the judgement call about how specific others need you to be**
Sometimes you need to be very specific in how you set objectives and at other times less so. This might be because the individual has expertise and experience or has done something similar many times before. In such a case they will probably be able to set the objectives with you very easily. As leader, you need to make the appropriate judgement call.

→ **Check the measures**
Make sure the measures and standards are relevant, appropriate and as clear as possible. Tried and tested methods of setting objectives measuring utilisation, sales revenue and realisation are things that are easy to measure, but may no longer be adequate. You may also need to include more sophisticated, qualitative metrics. This may include things like staff and client satisfaction scores, approval ratings, or customer/client feedback. Do the standards you are using for the person to whom you are allocating the work need to

change? Are you asking for a high enough standard? Or are you demanding impossibly high standards that set the individual up to fail?

→ **Consider using sub-objectives**
Think about breaking tasks into more than one task or into phases so you can use them for staff development purposes. However, this is not a licence to start micromanaging. The smart leader knows that checking in too much is a huge demotivator for smart professionals. They need the space to do the work their own way.

→ **Keep a record**
Keep a note for yourself of what has been agreed and how it was completed. You will need it when you contribute to performance review/feedback processes.

And remember

Setting objectives for other people is always tricky; handled badly, it risks demotivating high-performing teams. It presents you with three challenges. One is how to be clear about what you want and how to achieve it. The second is gauging your team's commitment to delivery; people are more committed when they have been able to make some contribution to an idea or task. Third, you need to take into account technical and professional knowledge and experience.

Always ask your people what they think they can achieve and how they might go about delivering it. Explain your expectations for what great task completion looks like and explore together what they think they can achieve. Involving team members in objective-setting also has the benefit of helping you to see if there are any shortfalls or misunderstandings, and areas for improvement.

Team dynamics

Teams made up of smart people can deliver outstanding results, so it is no surprise that every leader wants to build high-performing teams. Effective teams are often small in size, and need to be led and managed skilfully. The pay-off shows in the quality of the work they are able to deliver, which can, simply put, be outstandingly good. Really high-performing teams can be difficult to build and maintain but with the right personalities they can also be self-determining and require little support from a leader other than occasional check-ins and the provision of resources and air cover from the rest of the organisation. With the right people in place they not only deliver outstanding results, but make the work a joy too.

Building and leading teams need not be hard work. Most importantly, leaders need to pay attention to the human dynamics and human processes in the group. This also means having straight conversations about what is going on in the group – and not just about the work being done. Is everyone being heard? Are you listening to, and acting on, their suggestions? Smart people need to have their opinions sought and don't like being ignored. As the leader, be open to challenge and accept ideas contributed by your team members.

Example

Pablo smiled nervously as he looked around the work area his team inhabited. With the company growing so quickly, and new projects landing on his desk every week, it seemed that he was spending his whole time recruiting new people and allocating them to project teams. It was often tough to get the team dynamics right with so many people who hadn't worked together before. It was important that he deliver on tasks crucial to the organisation's growth and development; his highly talented team needed to establish ways of working together – and fast.

Maria, one of his more senior team members, suggested that it might help if she organised a team retreat to help everyone get to know each other better and to provide more context for the projects ahead. She deliberately organised the retreat to provide lots of 'together time'. The agenda covered opportunities for the group to examine and contribute to their future direction and how that would be measured; each team member had to share a skill or capability with their colleagues; they discussed and agreed how they would behave with each other and provide 'cover' for each other on their projects. All meals were taken together and although conversations continued late into the night, everyone was present and correct at the agreed time the next day. Pablo was there to talk more about their work and to support everyone, but he also gave people the space to get to know each other without him. As the retreat progressed there was a palpable sense of 'can-do' and accountability for each other growing in the team.

On their return to the office the difference was really tangible. The atmosphere was lighter, yet more purposeful, with a 'swagger' and air of confidence. This team were looking as though they could take on the world – and win.

Maria had been smart to recognise that the newly expanded team needed to spend time together to build the trust that would help them to succeed in a challenging environment. They had taken the time to find out about each other, to identify strengths and to create a safe space to admit where they might need help. Pablo would continue to provide clear direction, but he had a much better chance of delivering with a team who understood and trusted each other and had invested in their own success.

Do this

→ **See yourself as a team member
– even if you are not really**
Join in with activities as well
as managing them – but keep
in mind how your participation
is being viewed. There will
be times when it is good to
leave the team to itself. This
allows your 'deputies' and
the other leaders to exercise
their leadership when you are
absent on other occasions. And
remember it is always 'we' not
'I'; the team will be following
your example.

→ **Build trust**
Trust is the essential building
block for successful teams.
So be transparent about your
intentions: what you are trying
to achieve and the steps that
are going to be taken. And make
sure everyone on the team
knows too.

→ **Build psychological safety**
Make it safe for people to
challenge and be challenged.
One of your roles as a leader of
smart people is to create a safe
space to air disagreements so
that conflict can be surfaced
and resolved, and people who
are feeling vulnerable and

unsure are able to share their
concerns. The leader needs
to hear and deal with these
issues whilst at the same time
protecting the team members
who have made themselves
vulnerable by sharing their
concerns. Setting an example
that it is 'OK to be unsure and
to raise it' is vitally important.
Thereafter the leader needs
to work on resolving the
concerns and in such a way
that those who raised them feel
empowered and sympathetically
treated and the rest of the
team feel that progress and
momentum towards the
objectives are being maintained.

→ **Clear direction**
Get the team to contribute
to the direction of the task.
As a minimum they need
to have the opportunity to
question, challenge and make
a contribution to the overall
direction. The team needs to
understand the task. Once that
task has been clearly explained,
give your smart people as much
freedom as possible to get the
task done.

→ **Where you can, select new members carefully**

Always select new team members for capability and fit with the team and what you want to achieve. Then consider attitude and temperament. Include the team in the selection process for new members. Providing people have the capability, you can always add to their repertoire.

Most of the time we do not have the luxury of selecting our teams from scratch. But when the opportunity arises to add new members, bring in as much diversity to your team as possible. And when you have new members, pay careful attention to how they are integrated into the team. It requires due process and disciplined execution.

→ **Listen – lots!**

Yes really listen. Teams are made up of people, each with their own views, aspirations, fears and worries. The better you get to know your team, the more they will trust you and the more you will learn. Moreover, they will tell you how to make things better which will improve the teamwork and get a smarter result.

→ **Find real things to do**

Focus on the work in hand. The real work of team building happens on the job, doing the work together. Successful teams come together around the work, to achieve stuff. In some cases, teams can benefit from awaydays and team-building exercises, but these activities should always have a purpose, for example, helping a new team to get to know each other.

→ **Make time for the 'soft' stuff**

Groups that become teams do more than work together. They spend real time together. Certainly they work together, and they eat and travel together. They spend time talking and communicating together. And it doesn't really matter what they talk about. People build trust in each other through repeated interactions which enable them to predict each other's behaviour more accurately.

→ **Check how you are doing**

Have regular team reviews – what the military call 'After Action Reviews'. At regular junctures stop and ask: 'How are we doing?', 'What is going well?', 'What can we do better?', 'What should we be doing differently?', 'What do you need me to do more or less of?' etc. Listen well and then act on the ideas and suggestions wherever you can.

And remember

Teams need structure – and freedom. The leader's job is to provide them with both. Leaders also need to provide the necessary air cover so the team can get on with the job and get it done.

Our experience suggests that many professionals struggle to set a direction for their colleagues and subordinates. Yet having a clear direction is essential for teamwork – the team needs to know where it is going. And smart people need to have a contribution to that. Teams also need to agree their ground rules for how they will operate: what is set and what is negotiable.

When a team has done its job, really good teams celebrate together. It doesn't need to be big, expensive and flashy. But smart leaders know the importance of organising something that acknowledges and celebrates the team's achievements.

Remote teams

As the geographic reach of business increases, leaders are faced with the challenge of how to connect and empower smart people who are working remotely, in terms of distance and/or time. The trend is being driven by clients and customers, and technology is enabling what we once thought impossible; the expectation is that we can all work seamlessly in a connected world.

As diverse talent is distributed around the world, the ability to lead teams of remote knowledge workers is an increasingly important part of the leadership toolkit. By definition, working remotely means working without too much immediate, present supervision. We know that smart people have very clear ideas about how they think work should be organised and executed. Add to this limited opportunities for face-to-face communication and the increasingly blurred distinction between work and non-work in a world economy of ideas and knowledge, and the skill of leading smart people who work remotely is essential.

Example

Niels had the task of coordinating an international project team of people with diverse abilities and language skills. When he was chairing conference calls, hunched over the phone, head in his hands, eyes closed, he looked like deep concentration personified. When a colleague asked him if he was OK, the response was surprising. Apart from being oblivious as to his own behaviour, he confessed that he was concentrating so hard so that he could make sure he was summarising and reflecting the sentiments of the meeting.

Because of the differences in the fluency and vocabulary in the language of team members, Niels knew he needed to work hard to keep everyone engaged and on track. He made sure all documentation for each call was prepared and circulated well in advance. He scheduled the calls with local time zones in mind. During the meetings, he deliberately slowed the pace to involve everyone, check understanding and summarise contributions.

The project team had no idea of what was happening in Niels's office, or how he managed to keep the meetings moving so smoothly, but they were deeply grateful that he shouldered the responsibility to keep them engaged and involved. Needless to say, Niels's efforts ensured the diverse perspectives and views they all brought made a significant addition to delivering successful outcomes from his team who were, literally, scattered all over the world.

Do this

→ **Master your technology**
Learn to use technology, practise with it and get your IT people to help you get comfortable with it – whether that be instant messaging, WhatsApp, Skype, Zoom, FaceTime. Consider using these instead of email or phone calls – it really improves your presence and impact. You cannot expect your people to use the technology if you can't use it yourself.

→ **Meet face to face – or visit**
It may not be possible, but try to find ways to establish a personal connection. Visiting a remote office, can you engineer an extra day on your visit to meet remote workers, even if it is only for a tea or coffee? If you are on vacation near where a team member works, can you find an hour to meet them? If someone is visiting your location, make the time for a meal; 'Break bread with them.' Connect them to others in the team. If face to face is out of the question then have a one-to-one call using Zoom or Skype. This is especially important for new members of the team.

→ **Video or phone conference calls – go for equal treatment**
If you are hosting a call, either phone or video, then make sure *everyone* is using the technology. Resist the temptation to have a few people in an office and those who can't make it on the phone or video. It makes those *not* in the office feel disconnected. Either it's a call or it's not.

→ **Discipline**
Make sure boundaries are maintained. Start calls/meetings on time. (People may be waiting to go to bed or have got up early.) Finish calls on time. Get agendas and notes out promptly. As the leader, model the behaviour you expect of others. Smart people are invariably busy so will have lots of demands on their time. Prompt distribution of notes and minutes will help them manage their work more effectively.

→ **Share the 'pain'**
Think about the timing of your conference calls/meetings. It is almost certainly inconvenient for some of your colleagues somewhere. A call on your

Friday morning may be last thing on a Friday evening for your colleagues in Australia – perhaps not a great way to start their weekend. And your colleagues in the Middle East whose weekend is Friday and Saturday. And then there are national holidays and religious observances. Think about it.

→ Social is important

Social interaction is important for humans, so don't jump straight into the business of the call or meeting. At the beginning of the meeting or call, try getting people to 'check in'. Physically, where are they? What have they been doing that day? How are they feeling? If using videoconference – can they use their phone/laptop camera to show everyone their surroundings? Remember things like birthdays, national or religious celebrations, things that are important in *their* world. Help everyone realise the depth and breadth of who is on the call.

→ Agendas

When holding virtual meetings, make the agenda clear and make it a practice to circulate a draft in advance. Inviting shared contributions helps buy others into the final agenda and outcomes. What are the topics and expected outcomes? Are you using the call to make a decision, share information, air views, or hear from others? Allocate times to the items as best you can, and stick to them. Get the actual agenda out ahead of time so people can prepare.

→ Make it attractive

Make people really want to join your calls/meetings. Try rotating the chair, or note-taking, asking each constituency to share something about their country/office/location that others don't know. Make it fun. Take five minutes to have a personal check-in – share what is happening in their office or location. Try asking people how to make it the most important call in their calendar for that week. Make your call the one they will *not* miss!

→ Get as near to face to face as possible

When reaching out to your team, always try and 'scale' up. If you can meet face to face, great. If not, can you use video? If not, can you phone? Email and text are the very last resort. The fundamental thing is to find ways of connecting humans to humans as humans.

Defend and amplify

Most international companies have a global business language. Members of your teams may not be native speakers of that language. Your role as a leader is to make sure the less confident members are heard and to make space for their views if language is proving to be an issue. This is especially important for smart people who want to contribute and may find their own language limitations a personal frustration. Summarise and repeat for them. Listen for those who are *not* talking and carefully shut down those who are dominating the airwaves. Leaders sensitively make space for all of their team members.

And remember

Our experience tells us that working remotely – especially internationally – is not going to go away. We also know that leaders who can master this skill set really do reap rewards, both reputationally in terms of career and in getting results for their organisation. By harnessing different perspectives from different groups of smart people, leaders have a significant impact on the client deliverables.

Smart people know and understand the difficulties of coordinating across time and distance. They are often forgiving of leaders whose attempts to coordinate are uncertain or awkward, *providing the intention is clear*. So, the essence is lots of communication and investment of leadership and management time – probably much more than for local projects – and using every means available.

Working with different cultures

In an increasingly complex global world, the ability to work successfully with people from different backgrounds is critically important. Real skill in this area is a distinct performance differentiator. Even if your organisation is primarily domestic in nature, working with people from different cultures is almost inevitable, whether that be with your staff and teams, your clients, customers, intermediaries, suppliers or 'best friend' firms.

We know that clients increasingly value the ability to work seamlessly across borders and cultures. Research indicates that successfully addressing, reading, understanding, building relationships and communicating across cultures can increase productivity by as much as 26 per cent.

Example

Peter had built a very successful practice in his national home environment. He was selected to run an office in the UAE (United Arab Emirates). The team he inherited was made up of a range of professionals from different national cultures. As a leader he had been conditioned in his own national working culture for many years and all his leadership experience was on his 'home turf'. Suddenly the approach to leading and influencing that had served him well was not producing the same successful outcomes.

He learnt from his Swedish team members that they were motivated when he acted more as a facilitator among equals. However, his Indian and Chinese associates reacted better when he clearly set out and directed what he wanted done. For his Emirati colleagues the concept of maintaining face (or self-esteem) was at a depth that Peter had never imagined and was struggling to emotionally feel or understand. But he was smart enough to realise that it had to be fully observed and respected in order to motivate and achieve success. They were all different. Not wrong – just different. He quickly found that to succeed he would have to be very flexible and adaptable.

Success became more apparent to him when he started to look at the world through his colleagues' eyes: how they saw the world and made up their self-identity. To be a smart leader of a multicultural team, he realised that he needed to engage with them in their culturally preferred way and look at the world through their different frames of reference.

Do this

→ **Suspend your world view and assumptions**
Be aware that behaviours that to you are perfectly normal may seem odd to others. This can be difficult because it is often hard to think outside the box when you are in the box. Remember: when people act differently to you, it may not be right or wrong – just different.

→ **Be aware of your own unconscious cultural bias**
Think and be clear about your own cultural background. What are your 'rules of thumb' for dealing with situations? How might they be seen by others? Ask yourself, 'Do these still hold true and appropriate for this current set of circumstances?' If not, *you* need to adapt to be more effective.

→ **Interact with people and not stereotypes**
Start by assuming that people are acting with the best of intentions and with good rationale. Make that your default assumption. Recognise that everyone has good reasons for their behaviours and ways of thinking. Those reasons may not

be wholly visible to you; indeed they may not even look very sensible to you. But individuals do have good reasons – to their way of thinking – for the way they behave. People are people. Generalisations about people and groups at best distort and at worst deceive.

→ **Be curious and carry out your own cultural due diligence**
Find a reputable and reliable source of information and take the time to find out about the people with whom you are working. Do/don't do guides may seem simplistic but they do contain the occasional good idea. Identify someone who has recently been in the role you now find yourself in. Ask them for the few (three to five) key things you should know.

→ **Reflect and research others' cultural preferences**
Consider taking a short learning and development class to learn about others' culture. Are people from the culture you are to work with relationship- or task-orientated? And what are you? Should you spend time establishing commonality,

connectivity and respect before addressing the task or go straight into the task? Would you benefit from some adaptation of the natural approach in your culture?

→ **Be ready to adjust and adapt your 'normal' way of doing business**
This is not suggesting the loss of your ethical standpoint; rather, it means keeping the end point clearly in mind. How – and crucially when – you get there may well be less important, so long as you do actually get there. Practise alternating between your own and other styles, for example, between direct and indirect communication.

→ **Check your understanding**
Ask yourself: what have I just heard? What does it really mean? And does it mean what I think it means? Is there a subtlety in the wording, what is being said 'between the lines'? As a simple example: 'Let's table that item.' In the UK this means let's discuss it; in the USA it means let's *not* discuss it now. Smart people want to be understood, so checking will likely be welcomed, as well as clarifying things for everyone.

→ **Instil a comfortable pace**
Take more pauses and breaks to assist understanding, reflection and time for others to formulate a response. This is especially important where people may be communicating in a language that for them is their second or third language. This requires extra effort and is physically tiring as they have to adjust to listening to a different accent and vocabulary.

And remember

Smart leaders intuitively know that they need to take account of culture. They know that cultural DNA is part of what motivates, gives us our identity, and makes sense of our world. Ignoring culture is potentially damaging. It can lead to ongoing misunderstandings, misevaluations and misjudgements, and can damage relationships. It can also erode trust and damage reputations, sometimes irreparably.

Ignoring cultural nuances can seriously damage your business results at home and abroad. It can also seriously damage your reputation as a 'savvy' leader.

3.
Leading the Organisation

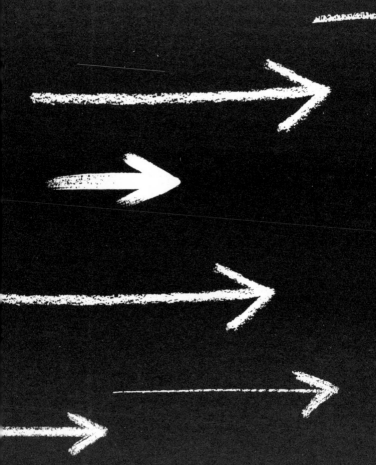

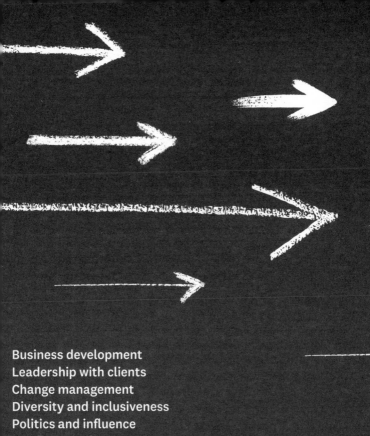

Business development
Leadership with clients
Change management
Diversity and inclusiveness
Politics and influence
Leading your boss
Leading your equals
Mentoring
Networking
Innovation and creativity
Managing stakeholders
Storytelling
Strategy
Vision

Business development

Selling your organisation's products and services – or your own services within the organisation – is an ongoing responsibility for leaders. External-facing teams expect to have a pipeline of work and internal-facing teams expect to be doing good work. In both cases they are looking for challenges that excite and test them.

Leading smart people means keeping them supplied with interesting work and at the same time helping them to develop the capability to 'sell' in their own right. To learn to do this, they will initially copy their role models as they begin to develop their own style and way of working. The need for their leaders to be out there – 'selling' in the broadest context – is imperative.

Example

In his mind, Kevin didn't sell – he was just incredibly curious about other people, their businesses and their issues. Yet Kevin was one of the best business developers in his organisation. By his own admission, Kevin hated selling – in fact, it was anathema to him. He could imagine nothing worse than visiting a client and trying to push products and services at them.

However, when he did visit clients and have conversations it was obvious that he was really good at assisting people, either by introducing them to his colleagues or by helping them buy services from his firm that would make a positive difference for them. One client commented: 'Kevin, you come and see me every six months for coffee and a conversation. You never try to sell me anything. So how come, three months down the line, I call you up and buy something?'

Kevin's philosophy was simplicity itself. Give prospects a 'gift' – a targeted free piece of information or advice or some small service – when you see them. It didn't need to cost much, but it was always thoughtful and relevant. He also wanted to work with clients he liked; it encouraged him to spend time with them, do a better job and have more fun, which in turn attracted others to the clients too. Kevin never worried about making his numbers – they just got better each year, simply fuelled by his curiosity and desire to help his clients over the long term.

Do this

→ **Stop selling**
Stop yourself, and your team, from chasing every immediate sale. Focus on building strong relationships that will deliver work for the long term. Recognise you may need to do some work free. Making 'gifts' is a powerful way of reinforcing your intent to make a difference and add value.

→ **Feed your pipeline**
Constantly look for opportunities to make or reinforce contact – but without making yourself a nuisance. Look for real opportunities when you are prospecting for business that your colleagues might be able to pursue. It is so much more powerful than taking colleagues 'on spec'.

→ **Use your network**
Map out your network: your external business contacts, industry contacts, college, neighbours and those inside the organisation. Make a point of feeding your network regularly. Your colleagues all need to know what you can do and how you can help them with their clients.

→ **Team meetings**
Have regular meetings with your team to share and sift opportunities they have identified. Teach them how to recognise and prioritise the best prospects.

→ **Improve your skills**
Practise 'facilitative selling' with your clients and prospects. This means thinking about the client first, what they need in relation to their strategy and agenda. It means using appropriate questioning to really understand them and then to position your service offerings in a way that specifically relates to their needs.

→ **Leverage junior staff**
Junior staff are often 'plugged in' to their peer associates across teams. Encourage associates to explore opportunities across specialisms and to develop innovative service offerings.

→ **Ask exploratory open questions**
'Who', 'what', 'where' questions give your client the opportunity to paint a picture for you of

what their organisation is doing, so that you can match their areas of need with your service offerings.

→ Remember you are talking to human beings

Start conversations with general pleasantries, but not for too long. Ask them about the issues they have and offer solutions to help them in their role and for their organisation. Make them look good.

→ Constantly evaluate your book of business

What is its value and how do you keep it topped up? Make sure you have key regular revenue earners as well as some larger opportunities. Smart people find it very easy to focus on the work in hand and this can become a good reason in their minds not to be out there generating business for the future. The current work becomes all-consuming at the expense of that crucial future pipeline.

→ Establish a sales rhythm

Do some business development every day, even if it is only a few minutes to send an email, share an article or follow up on social media. Choose the best time of day when you are fresh and uninterrupted, and book it in your calendar. Use technology and social media to update your newsfeeds for your sector and prospective clients.

→ Use your social media

Make sure your LinkedIn and other profiles are up to date. Follow up on notifications, for new jobs, anniversaries and articles, and do so personally. This is not a job that can be delegated.

→ Hunt in pairs

Find a colleague from another part of the business with whom you are comfortable working when visiting prospects and encourage your team to do the same. Plan the meetings carefully and identify the desired outcome from each of them. The aim of early meetings should be to get another meeting to continue the conversations.

After each meeting give each other feedback on how well each of you did. Remember: smart people can feel easily discouraged if meetings do not lead to immediate success.

→ Be distinctive with your prospects

Treat them as if they were already a client and follow up promptly with any agreed actions. People buy from people they know and like. So make yourself as agreeable as possible by engaging with them, for example, finding common areas of interest.

→ Get out more

Visit clients at their offices, tour their facilities, use their coffee shop, meet their colleagues. If possible visit their international offices too. Being physically present in a client's premises is a great way of getting to understand what is really going on in the organisation. And there is no substitute for visibility and being seen in the marketplace – it drives sales.

→ Involve your juniors

Get them to do preparatory work for clients and client meetings. Take them to meetings. It all contributes to their development. Make sure you give them feedback on how well they have done.

→ Evidence your relationships

Make a point of sending physical things (magazine articles, white papers, brochures, anniversary cards) to clients and customers on an ad hoc basis.

→ Follow up

Follow up within agreed timescales or as fast as possible to capture and consolidate the moment. Use the opportunity to suggest a next step and diarise for it.

→ Widen your contacts and prospective client network

Be generous and open with your own network. Making introductions to other potentially helpful contacts will make it easier to ask others to introduce you to people too. Reciprocity can be very powerful.

And remember

Business development skills have never been more important than in today's competitive world. Leaders need to understand the business development process for their organisation and ensure their teams are equipped to win business at every opportunity.

For leaders who are not in direct client service roles it is important their teams are aware of how the sales and business development functions operate so that they can respond swiftly to those who have that responsibility. For those of you leading internal functions, you need to make sure you are operating at the forefront of leading practice. Selling your ideas and initiatives internally in the organisation is also ever present.

Leadership
with clients

In most professional environments one of the first leadership roles that one undertakes is that of leading a client service team of other professionals. Success in leading a client service team is in part predicated on the nature of the relationship with the client. The better that relationship, the better the likely work opportunities and the more credibility that the leader has with their team. Clients value 'thought leaders' in their sector and want their adviser 'to make them look good'. Questions they may ask include 'Can my adviser add value through their knowledge of my needs?', 'Can s/he satisfy them?', and 'Can s/he help me and my organisation stand out?'

When clients speak to their advisers, they expect them to have a good understanding of business in general and their sector in particular. Corporate executives spend their lives immersed in their business and expect their advisers to have a good knowledge of the business, its markets and the issues it is facing. Obviously, they expect the professional to know something about their own area of expertise – mezzanine finance, real estate law, supply chain management etc. They also really value professionals who have an interest in them personally, not just as a client but as an individual too.

Your technical knowledge is important, but not enough. Through their more general business and industry expertise and knowledge, smart leaders see themselves as their clients' peer – not just as supporting technical specialists.

Example

Amita was a senior associate at a financial advisory firm. She was a solid technician who had, from an early stage, shown a keen interest in her clients and the sectors in which they operated. She took every opportunity to visit and hold meetings at her clients' offices and to learn more about how they operated. Having that knowledge built her credibility with clients and demonstrated her interest in them. It meant that, whenever she received instructions, she could constructively question their objectives for the transaction and contribute ideas and insight into its implementation. Clients were impressed by the value her knowledge and understanding added to their own thought processes and risk assessments.

As a result, a particular board director at one of her clients requested that Amita should always be on the team for his transactions. This led to an increased number of instructions, and, at times, Amita was seconded to the client's business development team. It enhanced the client's business and also Amita's interest and position in her firm. It led to deeper and better relationships with the client, recommendations to other companies and independent references in industry directories. She was deservedly fast-tracked to partnership ahead of her peers.

It was summed up for Amita when she overheard the client director saying to one of his colleagues, 'All corporate financiers know finance. We need financiers who understand our business. Why can't we have more financiers like Amita?'

Do this

→ **Get yourself business-'savvy'**
Find time to study business. Enlist the help of your business development team or your learning and development team. Attend a programme or class. Sign up for a distance-learning module or MOOC (Massive Open Online Course). For most professionals, early career development is centred around acquiring the necessary technical skills to do the 'work'. However, as careers progress, business knowledge and people skills make all the difference; they will give you an edge.

→ **Take a real interest in an industry or sector**
Pay attention to what you are reading. You only have a limited amount of time so focus your reading/updating time on the sector that is your 'major'. To make it easier, task one or two of your team with reading periodicals and journals and ask them to precis relevant articles.

→ **Ask the 'right' questions about your clients**
What is their key revenue earner? What is their competitive position and edge? Who are their key competitors? Why are they winning or losing in the market? What is the impact of new advances in technology or regulatory changes? Start thinking as broadly as you can about their business. If you were an executive in the client's business, what would you be worrying about?

→ **Stay up to date with the client's business**
Check your newsfeeds every day for things that impact your client. Are their shares on the move? Why? What are the implications for the client – both as an organisation and as a person? Have they personally made or lost money? Has a hostile bid been launched? Have new regulations come into play? Your clients live and breathe these issues daily. If you want to be seen as the leader amongst their preferred service providers you need to live and breathe them too.

→ **Generate insights**
Generate insights based on a thorough understanding of the client's business. Read up on your client's business and

feed that into your own toolkit. Start with a PESTEL (Political, Economic, Social, Technological, Environmental and Legal) analysis to get to grips with the important factors in a sector; use Porter's Five Forces model to understand industry dynamics, the Value Chain to identify how a business creates value. Speak to your business development professionals, get them to advise you and extend your understanding. What are the implications of the things you are reading and seeing? What will they mean for your client? What would you do if you were part of the client's leadership team?

→ Become a 'friend in business'

Invest time in things outside the actual work you are doing for the client. Have conversations about your main contact's career, objectives and relationship with their boss. Share your insights about what else you are seeing and hearing in the marketplace. Do the things you would do with and for a friend. The principles of becoming a friend in business are the same as with your non-work friends: show interest, find common interests and follow through.

→ Get off the fence

Have a view or opinion about the issues of the day. If a client asks what you think about X, Y or Z, they are expecting you to have an informed view. They are *not* expecting you to make decisions for them. Nor are they worried if you caveat your comments so it is clear that you are not offering advice. But your client is expecting an informed comment or a view. Make sure you can do so.

→ Ensure business understanding

Educate your junior staff in the principles of business from a very early stage in their careers. Your organisation's learning and development curriculum should include programmes and material to support them throughout their careers.

And remember

All the best client handlers we have ever met have taken the time to learn about their clients through a lens of business, not just their own technical specialism. They all have a very deep understanding of their clients' business fuelled by a deep sense of curiosity.

This enabled them to have serious conversations that moved them from the role of a technician to being a serious player who was always welcome in the boardroom. They achieved the often-talked-about, but elusive, status of being a real trusted business adviser, the 'go-to person' for the client when they have an issue. At the same time, they were also important role models for their teams, modelling client leadership behaviours crucial to their people's personal development.

Change management

Smart leaders know that the world is changing – and changing fast. Business models are changing more rapidly than ever before with new, disruptive technologies and alternative business models appearing ever more quickly. It truly is the new 'normal'. As a leader you have to respond quickly to changes in your marketplace or risk losing competitiveness. You can either deal with changes reactively – by responding only when absolutely required, which will probably be too late; or you can be proactive – by anticipating change and taking a competitive position. Both courses will impact the people involved and likely require them to make changes too.

Humans differ in their reactions to change. Some find it uncomfortable and seek ways to resist. Others welcome it because of the intellectual stimulation and challenge that goes with the prospect of the new. In professional service firms, and organisations with very bright people, the fact that people get bored easily is a great help to the leader.

To lead change successfully you need to build a strong case for why things need to be different. Potential impacts need to be identified and analysed. You'll need buy-in from stakeholders and other leaders, seeking their contributions at the very beginning and addressing any concerns they may have.

Once built and agreed, the plan needs to be communicated widely. After that the leader's role is to get out of the way so the people can run it, providing and enabling support, information, knowledge, skill and training throughout the organisation. The leader's role then becomes one of monitoring progress and deciding if and when the plan might need to be amended.

Example

Nalini had been appointed to be the managing director of a newly merged boutique corporate finance house. Both organisations had been under a lot of stress recently; they had lost ground to their competitors and had started to acquire the reputation for being slightly out of touch. The merger was just the start of the changes Nalini knew that she would have to make for the new company to survive and thrive.

Knowing from experience that change is often difficult, she appointed change champions. She selected them from first-line management and influential line managers; she picked some who embraced change and others whose initial resistance was overcome by being appointed. She then ensured that she and her change team established visible 'early wins' to start to embed and create the new reality of the change. These included jointly bidding for and winning new business, encouraging everyone 'just to muck in' even before the new structure had bedded down.

Alongside these quick wins, Nalini knew a key task was to tackle staff anxiety and insecurity. There was nothing for it but a clearly structured road map with a lot of hard work. Based on previous experience, she prepared a comprehensive communications plan. It included a Q&A for heads of business areas to use for briefings and information for major stakeholders. She communicated with international offices via the intranet and videoconferencing, setting dates for her to visit in person. Communications outlined and discussed her vision, the potential benefits of changes to operations, and dates of briefing meetings. A confidential channel was set up to solicit suggestions for improvements. She visited all offices personally to lead town hall meetings, and addressed colleagues' concerns sympathetically.

Nalini was smart to identify that lasting change does not just happen and that buy-in and engagement are key to its success. This takes time and effort, but she knew that they were absolutely necessary to create the smooth transition everyone needed. And she also knew it had been more than worthwhile when the new organisation started to win new clients and a new-found reputation for dynamism and innovation.

Do this

→ **Start with the people**
The ultimate success of any change depends upon how well colleagues embrace and engage with it. Be very clear about the impact on them and help them become comfortable with what is and will be happening. They need to understand what it means for them and the why – the benefits that the change will bring.

→ **Create and share your vision**
Involve others in creating the vision. This is especially important with smart people whose engagement and contribution are essential to successful implementation. Change management needs a clear endgame to encourage the active engagement of the people affected. People need to be able to add to the vision and make it their own.

→ **Allow adequate time**
Lasting change takes time. Be realistic in your change management planning about the timescales for the proper engagement you'll need to change the hearts and minds of your smart colleagues.

→ **Use multiple change strategies**
Leading change with smart people is invariably an organic process; only so much can be driven down from the top. It requires an ongoing process of engagement to secure input, ideas and energy from the people who are getting the work done on a day-to-day basis. Leaders need to think through and understand the consequences, and likely outcomes, of their chosen strategies.

→ **Make it real**
Make change obvious, visible and grounded in the day-to-day work as soon as practicable. It needs to be seen and felt in the actual work that people are doing day to day. Smart people need to see that things really have changed or they will likely dismiss the efforts as 'yet another' failed attempt at change.

→ **Take risks**
Involvement is usually much better than a push-down approach. However, this means that the outcomes are also less certain. So, if things don't

always work out – as they won't – see it as learning and not a failure.

→ Spread it wide

Make sure what has been tried, tested and found to work is shared across other parts of the operations quickly. Don't reinvent the wheel.

→ Build capacity

Find ways of increasing the amount of capacity in your work groups so your people can make the necessary changes. This may mean getting more people, money, finding time by stopping doing some tasks, accessing needed tools and equipment. Too often efforts at change fail because they are under-resourced and existing teams are unable to take on the new work because they are still overloaded by their old responsibilities.

→ Resist the urge to give the 'answer'

Don't assume that only those at the top have good ideas. Encourage people to take responsibility by sharing the end goal and inviting their ideas, suggestions and thoughts about how best to get there. Assuming the suggestions are sensible, support their ideas with resources and your time. If you are not sure, coach them to ensure you understand both the upside and the risks. At the same time don't shy away from taking decisive action when your judgement tells you to provide the answer yourself.

→ Communicate like never before

Use every opportunity to share the message about the destination to which you are heading and – especially for smart people – why you are heading there. Be clear on the destination but very flexible about the journey; the all-important thing is the end point and getting everyone there as quickly and safely as possible. If you are starting to feel sick of hearing yourself, that is probably a good thing. Keep on keeping on!

→ Use all available media to communicate across the whole organisation

A clear vision of the end state has to be fully understood and shared. Exploit all media across your organisation: town halls, intranet, emails, newsletters, videoconferencing. Do everything to get the vision across and instil a sense of purpose and mission in colleagues.

→ Empower the extroverts and the introverts

Make sure you seek opinions from those who may not otherwise speak up. Anonymous surveys are one route and can counter those who resist with the loudest voices. Remember: quiet people may turn passive-aggressive if they feel their voice has not been heard.

→ Find and work with 'change champions'

Appoint people as 'change champions' or into roles where they are given time to lead initiatives, trials, projects or piloting new ways of working. Building a distributed network with many people making lots of small, coordinated changes can deliver a big result in a short timescale. Change champions should be chosen from people at all levels in the organisation, especially where they have intrinsic knowledge of systems, culture, operations, people and processes. The main criteria are their willingness and ability to make change happen.

→ Dealing with blockers and resisters

'Call out' those who are blocking or resisting. Sometimes all it takes is some feedback to support behaviour change or to turn resistance into support. As a matter of principle, give people the benefit of the doubt; there may be good reasons for their resistance and blocking. And bear in mind that if you do encounter resistance, one way of overcoming it is by recruiting early resisters as change champions.

→ Removing blockers

There may come a time when you need to remove those who are persistent or wilful in obstructing the changes you are making. This may mean reassignment to another part of the organisation or, in a worst-case scenario, dismissal. The manner in which you handle the removal communicates a very powerful message and will be heavily scrutinised, so it needs to be done respectfully and aligned with the organisation's values. This really has to be the very last resort, when everything else has failed.

→ Learn and develop as you go – be flexible

Keep a clear view on the final destination, but be flexible on how you get there. The best-laid plans and programmes will inevitably need modification as things unfold. Leading through change creates many new and unexpected challenges. Your success will depend upon your skills in learning and adjusting to unexpected challenges. Make change permanent by comparing the old with the new, identifying key lessons learnt, and by celebrating improvements brought about by the change.

And remember

The ease or difficulty in making change happen depends on the way the people involved are treated. When involved, engaged and invited to be part of a process where their concerns and issues are listened to and dealt with and they have a part in co-creating the final state, people can be incredibly creative, enthusiastic and energised. Treat them poorly and do things 'to' them and it becomes a surefire recipe for disaster.

The smart leader's role is to provide a context that ensures maximum engagement and 'buy-in' to the proposed changes. You need to provide as much clarity, reassurance and psychological safety as possible. Paint a picture of a more interesting, exciting, fun future while being honest and transparent about the journey.

Diversity and inclusiveness

Well-led diversity and inclusiveness programmes are good for business – internally and externally. High-performing, inclusive, diverse teams make a positive difference to the bottom line. They are more creative, more responsive and deliver better client service. Simply put, a systemic or programmatic focus on diversity and inclusion has real commercial benefits: it improves the quality of staff recruitment, engagement, productivity and retention which can give you a real competitive edge.

From a leader's point of view, diverse teams can be more demanding because of the challenge from different perspectives, but they are also a lot more fun to lead. Smart leaders strive for diversity and inclusion at all levels of their organisations and seek to change attitudes and culture so that inclusiveness is normalised.

Example

ABC Co. responded to a renewal request for one of their biggest contracts: a multi-year annuity that was enjoyed by the staff and delivered good profits for the company. The pitch process proceeded without drama. The proposal was submitted in accordance with the procurement instructions. The champagne was put on ice while they waited expectantly for confirmation that the contract would be extended for another three years.

There was a deep sense of shock when the news broke that they had lost the contract. The contract was awarded to an upstart competitor. The prices and service levels were similar. There was little sense that they might have run their bid differently. The team was solid, the track record was acceptable, and there was the history. So how come they had lost it?

The post-award review revealed that the purchaser had changed in significant ways since the last renewal. The new contract winner had forensically monitored and studied the buyer's new business reality and had gone to great lengths to make the case for change based on how they presented themselves at the final presentation. This included team mix and the style and mode of presentation. They carefully matched their team to the client and the markets in which it operated in terms of gender, race and ethnicity, as well as their dress and level of formality.

In contrast, ABC Co. looked and felt old-fashioned and out of step with how the buyer and the industry in which they operated had changed. They had mistakenly taken for granted that just doing 'the same as always' would be enough to win them the business and seriously underestimated how prevailing cultures had moved on.

Do this

→ **Take a long hard look at your team**

Identify your regular work colleagues. How many are older than you? Younger than you? A different colour from you? From a different country or ethnic grouping? Religion? LGBT? Is your team diverse in terms of the organisational ranks/grades that you have represented? Ask yourself what constituency views are missing and how you might add to them. Over time, start injecting new people into the team. And if it is not possible to bring them onto the team (really?), then find ways of obtaining their insights and contributions from a more diverse pool. By any standards, having too many people who are 'alike' in any team is not a good thing.

→ **Take a really good look at your clients**

How diverse are the executives with whom you regularly interact? Can you reach out to others to get different perspectives? Are you dealing with the same group the whole time? What can your clients learn from how you are leading on diversity and inclusion? Engage in the debate with them. Ask about their efforts and what they are doing. Offer suggestions to help them based on your experience and leadership.

→ **Use your awaydays and meetings to reinforce your messages**

Bring in visitors from other departments or other organisations to offer challenging viewpoints. But be vigilant to make sure you have not just invited people in your own image. Or simply something out of 'left field' in order to stimulate the questions 'How might this apply to us?' or 'What can we learn from this?' Instead of using familiar formulae for your events, give the responsibility for organising to different team members with the remit to bring in something new and different. And don't forget to have the conversation afterwards, asking 'So, what do we know now that we didn't know earlier?' or 'What have we learnt from our experience today?' – and be sure to listen to everyone's view.

→ Bring different thinking and perspectives to your team

Think, where do you get your new ideas from? How often are you attending conferences, think-tank meetings? Gatherings at universities or those given by other institutions or sectors? Make a point of at least once a month going to an event or function where you will see, hear, experience something new and meet people who are not your usual group of contacts. Try taking a junior member of your team with you to get their perspective.

→ Challenge your assumptions

As a leader you have a behaviour repertoire that has made you successful. That repertoire is built on a series of assumptions and unconscious responses to situations. Now is the time to question the basis of those assumptions. What criteria do you use for selecting team members: someone like you or someone very different? It's easy to make these decisions on autopilot. Stop and think instead. You have the power to include in your team people who are different.

→ Own the messages

Find your own words and ways of communicating and executing the agenda. Leading with behaviour that people have come to expect from you provides authenticity to the delivery of your messages. Smart people know when they are being 'spun' – and they know when their leaders are just parroting the corporate 'party' line.

→ Pay attention to the 'small' stuff

Much discrimination is not intentional and occurs as micro-inequities, for example, not inviting quieter, less confident group members to speak. This sort of group dynamic needs as much attention as the formal content and decision-making that are the overt subject of the meeting. The smart leader pays attention to who does most of the speaking and makes space for others: the one who hasn't said a word and needs to be invited to speak, the one who looks worried or fearful and needs you to reassure them. Make sure they are heard. Smart people notice these little touches and expect them from their leaders.

And remember

Diversity and inclusiveness is a real business issue that is becoming ever more important. Increasingly, client proposal documents ask for details of the 'mix' of the proposed team: whether it includes minorities, represents the wider population etc. Some clients want to know how their professional advisers are making efforts to improve their diversity.

Even if the clients don't ask about your diversity and inclusiveness efforts, tell them. It puts you on the front foot and is a great opportunity to create differentiation in the marketplace. Being able to answer client questions about diversity and inclusion with accuracy and great practical examples is becoming essential. Not just because it makes for good leadership; it's also the right thing to do.

Politics and influence

As a leader your role is to get things done to improve the capability of your organisation or firm and to support long-term sustainability. It is not just about pursuing your own needs or those of your team. As a leader you have an organisation-wide remit.

Every organisation is a complex network of interlocking systems of influence – or politics. The reality is that, as a partner or leader in a firm, you are at the heart of the politics. Politics is simply the process of exercising influence and is essential for you as a leader, both of your client teams and among your peers.

Trying to avoid 'politics' is not an option. It will simply see you marginalised and pushed to the edges of the business. It will affect your ability to attract the people and resources you need to service your clients and achieve your own agenda. Ultimately that will affect your status and reputation as a client handler. Appropriate, ethical use of the political process in the organisation is essential for long-term career success and should always be about the greater good of the institution and its people.

Example

Mandavi was a managing associate who had lived in different countries from an early age and had a natural affinity for working across borders. He had started at his law firm as a trainee. He was ambitious; with focus and hard work, and by learning from the right people, he hoped to build experience and a profile to make a career to partner.

The firm had some limited international work. Mandavi felt there was potential to expand into these markets more aggressively. He was keen to be part of this and kept making suggestions, building up a network of contacts, and boosting the firm's profile in the most attractive markets.

Some of the firm's partners supported Mandavi's efforts, but as he started to gain some traction, attracting clients and work to the firm, he hit a roadblock. Marty, a senior partner of the firm and self-appointed gatekeeper for international work, started to criticise and undermine Mandavi's work and deny him the resources he needed to build on his initial success. Marty also led a 'whispering campaign' against Mandavi and his prospects. As Marty was politically very powerful in the firm, this was a major obstacle to Mandavi's ambitions.

Overall, Mandavi was happy at the firm and had made some good friends and supporters. He remained convinced of the opportunities for international expansion. He reflected on his position and spoke to a couple of supportive partners for advice. As a result, he decided upon a strategy to try to unblock the situation in which he found himself. He decided to share with other partners the international opportunities that were being created, including those that would benefit Marty directly. In time, he created a coalition which supported his work, but also helped Marty to expand his part of the international practice and his profile. It was not always easy but being politically aware and understanding how influence worked in his firm, Mandavi was able to develop a successful career, while the firm also benefited from increased billings and profile in international markets.

Do this

→ **Change your mindset**
Recognise politics and influence as the way things are done in organisations. This is especially true in partnerships. Remember: people do things for what, to them, are very good reasons, even if you don't either understand or agree with them. The more you understand the real motives behind others' actions, the more you'll understand the process of influence in your firm.

→ **Make sure you, and your motives, are trusted**
Be explicit; share your intentions and motives with your people. One leading view is that trust is built when you are explicit about your motives, doing what you say you were going to do, and then repeating it time after time. Repetition breeds certainty; inconsistency fosters uncertainty and doubt. Strong leaders know that smart people have very low tolerance thresholds for dealing with inconsistent behaviour.

→ **Get good at 'reading' your organisation or firm**
Find out who seems to get things done effortlessly. And find out why. What is the key to their success? How and when do they engage with colleagues and other influencers? Who speaks with whom, when, where, about what? Are you included in those meetings? Which meetings do you need to attend? How can you get yourself invited and become part of the agenda?

→ **Be aware of your reputation and associations**
Get a very clear understanding of your reputation. Self-awareness is key – are you seen to be aligned to a particular group? If so, are these the groups with whom you wish to be associated? Do you need to cultivate other connections or make changes to your reputation? Does your reputation need to change?

→ **Changing your reputation**
Decide what in the future your reputation needs to say about you. What behaviour do others want to see? What work assignments, projects or task forces will provide the opportunities for you to behave differently, so that others will speak about you in a different way? This is not a 'one and

done'; this is potentially a long-term piece of work. Those who are observing you will be watching for a pattern of behaviour to emerge.

→ Increase your sources of influence
Increase the number of ways you are able to influence others. When push comes to shove, what do you rely on as your sources of influence? Association with a client? Your personal style and personality? Your ability to reward – or punish? By connection to a powerful sponsor?

Leaders rarely rely on just one source so having more sources of influence to call upon is always useful.

→ Walk your talk
Make sure your behaviour is consistent with your stated intentions. There is an old expression that action speaks louder than words – and contradictions howl. Inconsistencies stand out as warning signals that all is not as it seems; and can undermine the trust others may have in you.

→ Make sure everything you do is for the 'greater good'
Make sure your actions are clearly seen as for the benefit of the whole firm rather than just in your personal interest. Your subordinates, colleagues and peers are all acutely aware of how you are spending your time and will be making judgements about whether your actions are for the greater good.

→ Build coalitions
Seek out others who have similar views about the longer-term future of the organisation. Ideally identify those who have the necessary influence and find ways of becoming part of their network of influence in the firm. In your coalitions, work up joint plans of action to further an agenda for the good of all. Expand and share your networks so that your combined influence bases are broadened.

→ Expand your networks
Volunteer for firm-wide projects, initiatives and activities. These are not only important tools to demonstrate your commitment to the wider firm; they also expand your network. A key tool for influencing in densely networked, influence-driven organisations – like professional service firms – is your network of contacts. Anything you can do to extend the breadth and depth of your networks will extend your ability to get things done and also your influence.

And remember

Politics in organisations are neither good nor bad. But they are a fact, simply the way people use their influence to get things done. Be clear about your own motivations and purpose. A big part of your ability to influence is the behaviour you choose to use in pursuit of your political agenda.

You need to model behaviour that reflects your organisation's values. Values are intended to guide people when things are unclear or uncertain. Leadership often means taking people to places where things need to be done differently, or are new, unclear or ambiguous. Living your organisation's values enables you to model appropriate behaviour for everyone.

Most of the professionals we know are clear that they want to leave their organisation in a better, stronger state than it was before they became a leader. They know that will be their legacy. Your ability to build a legacy is clearly linked to your ability to influence the organisation. You won't be able to understand how to improve your own ability to get things done and leave a legacy if you don't understand how to tap into the current channels for influence.

Leading your boss

Leading your boss may sound like an oxymoron – but it is an essential skill if you are to lead smart people successfully. We are not talking about crude and simplistic manipulation but a process of supporting and positively influencing your boss for the good of everyone.

Your people expect you to represent their views, to procure the necessary resources for their work, and generally to look after their interests and well-being. Inevitably your organisation will have limited resources in terms of cash, person power, access to materials and facilities. One of the measures of your success as a leader is how well you are able to access the resources needed to achieve your agenda, which usually means a strong working relationship with your boss, one based on respect and trust. This respect and trust will be earned and built through regular interaction. You will probably need to take the lead on this, so build this into your schedule and always look out for opportunities to build this key relationship.

Example

An international organisation had just acquired a new business. The board soon realised that the acquisition was in a far worse state than they had originally understood. It was dominated by a leader who ran it as his personal fiefdom and domain – and would not stand for any questioning or challenge to his authority or decisions.

A new leader, Emily, was appointed from outside. She brought in a whole new team, one of whom, Magdalena, was appointed head of Legal and HR Services. Magdalena's first task was to make an assessment of the current Legal and HR organisations and present it to Emily, ready for the parent company's board meeting in six weeks' time.

Magdalena duly did this and in addition went well beyond her brief to provide three viable options for the next steps to make the integration work. She also provided some well-received help to the Finance Director in reviewing his function. One of Magdalena's recommendations for Legal and HR was selected by the board and, as a result, the integration process was expedited by two months. This led not just to the success of the acquisition but also to the production of a blueprint which was used as a case study internally to inform how to make a success of future acquisitions.

As a result Magdalena's reputation and career grew markedly and she became sought after as a key internal 'troubleshooter' in the company. It had also helped to reinforce Emily's position with the board. By demonstrating proactivity, reliability and creativity, Magdalena repaid in spades the faith Emily had shown by bringing her in to head up a key team at a crucial time for the organisation.

Do this

→ **Keep them informed**
Make a point of having regular catch-up meetings so your boss knows that you are on top of your agenda. And be sure to include a conversation about how the business is doing more broadly. What's working, what's not and how your part of the business might help resolve issues and problems elsewhere.

→ **Always take solutions**
When you have an issue or problem that you need to refer upwards – always take two options or possible solutions with you. And make sure you have a preferred option from those that you take. Your boss may have a different 'take' on the problem but they will also know that you have thought it through carefully and just need help in making the right judgement call.

→ **Be available**
Book some 'chaos' time in your schedule every week. This doesn't need to be a lot – an hour will do, but protect it. This will give you the capacity to respond to crises when they occur. If no crises occur you will

have a time 'bonus' each week that you can use for your own development or to make some headway into other projects or long-term plans.

→ **Volunteer**
Offer to take tasks on for your boss. And be specific. Don't just offer 'Anything I can be doing?' Pick things that (a) will make a difference, (b) you believe you can do well, and (c) things from which you will learn.

→ **Drive the relationship**
Take responsibility for making update meetings, briefings etc. If you want time with your boss, go about finding the time slots. Think about inviting him or her to your team meetings, awaydays, leaving parties or new-joiners meetings from time to time so that they can stay connected to your smart people.

→ **Be proactive**
Get stuff done ahead of time. There will be certain things that you know will happen: the annual budget and performance management cycles are two simple examples. You know when they are due, so plan and

get them done on time. Your boss really does have better things to do with their time than chasing you for stuff you should have delivered already.

→ Be reliable

Always deliver – on time, every time. You know that one thing which drives you mad is when people don't honour their commitments. Like you, your boss will have a series of dependencies they will be coordinating. Non-delivery of projects or work invariably has systemic implications elsewhere in the organisation. Don't be a cause of irritation and delay.

→ Be absolutely trustworthy

Stay above the office gossip, 'rumour mill' and negative politics. Being a leader can be a lonely place and trusted confidant(e)s who can respect and maintain confidences can be tough to find. One way of doing this is to build a reputation for never casting aspersions, and treating everyone equally and respectfully. Never saying a bad word about colleagues and being upbeat is a good way to start.

And remember

This advice is tough. Basically we are saying that you need to find ways of taking on even more work into your already busy schedule. But we offer this advice with good reason. Your boss is just like you – overloaded – so offers of competent, reliable help will almost certainly be welcomed. Find ways of helping him or her by sharing the load – but not in a sycophantic way.

Remember that your motive is to make the enterprise stronger and better; it is not to position yourself to take over from your boss. That may be an eventual outcome, but must never, ever be your primary rationale. If you think about it, there are other good reasons for helping your boss aside from building a better, easier working relationship. Can you think of a better way to prepare yourself for future promotion, to learn more about the business and extend your own networks and influence base?

Leading your equals

Leading people who are your technical peers requires a continuous process of encouraging, influencing and persuading – and doing so in such a way that they willingly forgo things they want to do, in order to work with you for a common good.

In many professional organisations leaders are often elected by their peers. The outward perception is that everyone is equal and the managing partner, team leader or senior counsel is *primus inter pares*. That's not always the reality. But how do you lead your peers? They are smart, successful, capable professionals who tend to resent anyone restricting their 'freedoms', especially those related to being entrepreneurial or that might influence how they run their portfolio or projects. They will all have individual agendas, whether publicly disclosed or not. Yet the success of the organisation is dependent upon all of them working in unison and walking together in the same direction.

Example

Jenny, the CEO of an organisation made up of research scientists, needed someone to lead a new initiative for the company. She had already had one false start: the person she had initially chosen to take the reins had proved unequal to the task, and the project was currently going nowhere. She needed the right person to step up to steady the ship.

Selecting the right person would not be easy. All of the candidates had the right scientific background and experience, but she also needed someone who could show direction, encourage commitment and lead by example. After taking soundings, the overall consensus was that it should be Carole.

Jenny was not disappointed. Carole – a top researcher in her own right – knew better than anyone that stepping up to lead a team of her clever and competitive peers was not going to be straightforward, so was aware of the pitfalls from the start. Her time working outside the scientific community in business development and marketing had taught her the importance of setting clear objectives and the power of working consensually. She had also recently invested some personal development time to learn more about coaching.

Delivering the new initiative would need everyone on board, so Carole's starting point was to involve her peers in her plan for implementation. Throughout the project she made sure she kept in touch so that everyone had the support and resources they needed to get the job done. She was generous in allocating the most prestigious research tasks. When, at one point, one of the phases went less well, she kept her cool and made the key decisions needed to get everything back on track. In short, she showed leadership, stepping up and modelling the kinds of behaviours that won her credibility and respect, and enabled her both to deliver the new initiative on time and to budget, and to boost the reputation of the whole team.

Do this

→ **Remember someone has asked you to do the job because they think you can do it well**
Do you know why? What has been seen, what is it that has made you stand out as the person who is best placed to lead your peers? What is/are the source(s) of your credibility? What is the basis of that respect and credibility?

→ **Make sure everyone knows that whatever you are doing, you are doing it for the good of the whole firm, not for self-aggrandisement, or to build your own reputation**
People follow others they believe are going somewhere, so where are you planning on taking things? What is your agenda? Have you consulted to make it an inclusive initiative that can be delivered through a process of genuine engagement?

→ **Shift your focus; your job now is to make your peers successful**
How can you best help and support your peers so that they are successful? Find out and do what you can to remove barriers that might be blocking them.

Make sure you represent their interests – both individually and collectively – and if possible let it be known that you are so doing. At the same time remember that you are also a member of a body corporate, which also has expectations of you. Fixing what you can is essential even if it seems trivial to you. And remember it is also important to ensure you are aligned with current corporate initiatives so as to retain the confidence of your leaders.

→ **Remember – it is *not* about you – it is about them**
Develop coaching skills and learn to use them subtly. Get to know – really know – your peers, their strengths, things they need help with. Offer support, and coach them, in a variety of subtle ways to help them succeed. This is all about making the judgement calls about who needs help and how best to deliver that help.

→ **Use the organisational levers at your disposal**
Every firm has 'levers' that usually operate in cycles: the budgeting round, the

performance appraisal round, off-sites, conferences, reviews, hiring etc. Your team expect you, as the team leader, to do these things. All these occasions provide opportunities for you to be seen as a leader. The challenge is how you use the opportunities. Remember you will be closely scrutinised and compared, and need to use them with integrity and without being seen as manipulative or as an opportunist.

→ Use the power of symbolism and ritual

Pay attention to the things celebrated in the office and how you celebrate. Find and use other rituals and symbols that exist in your team or organisation. Discern what messages these are giving others. When someone joins your group, leaves, wins something or loses a pitch, how do you respond – what do you do? Everyone else is watching to see if you act like their leader 'should' in their terms. Similarly what symbols do you have? Awards – even jokey ones – tell a message. Evaluate what you have, change what you need to, stop others and institute new ones. Rituals are prime leadership opportunities where, as the leader, you are able to

make a powerful statement about who you are as a group and what you stand for.

→ Be alive to opportunities to demonstrate leadership

Being a leader means 'stepping up' and displaying courage when unplanned situations arise and people are not sure what to do. It means showing the way. It means going into the uncertain or unknown. Not for self-aggrandisement, but to help your colleagues. Often these situations just occur so having a 'servant' focus on your colleagues and how you can help them at all times will help make these occasions more obvious.

→ Give up stuff

Relinquish some of your cherished tasks, fun jobs or things you have kept as you do them well or enjoy them. They might be powerful developmental experiences for others in your team. Really good leaders give up things in order to make others better.

→ You have limited resources – use them all

Act as a role model. Be very aware that you are judged, in part, by the company you keep. The colleagues you lunch with, meet with, projects you are personally involved with. Your peer group will make judgements about you as they see you as a member of those groups. Ensure you maintain and nurture your sources of credibility and increase the support and challenge you give to others. Finally, be sure to use the organisational mechanisms that enable you to give feedback to your people.

And remember

Your success when leading smart professionals is, paradoxically, based on the judgements your peers make about how good a team member you are. They are constantly making an evaluation about whether you are playing for the good of the entire team. Subconsciously they are also making a judgement about how much help you are giving them and how much you might be trying to constrain and impinge on their freedom to act. It can be a difficult balance to strike. Perhaps the question really good leaders ask is 'How would I react if I were on the receiving end of my behaviour?' and the answer to that question guides their actions.

Remember your colleagues are constantly judging how good you are as a leader, by how good a team member you are amongst your peer groups. They will make that judgement call based on what sort of follower you are. So careful reflection upon how you would want to be led is essential.

Mentoring

Mentoring is an advisory relationship with a colleague that is usually about longer-term career options and career development. It is an opportunity to raise work, career, organisational and sometimes even personal issues confidentially, and to seek advice on how to handle them. For many professionals and knowledge workers, their day-to-day work involves the application of experience, applying a high level of technical application and judgement to cases that might look similar but are rarely identical in terms of context and circumstance. This is where a mentor can add huge value by bringing to a mentee those extra years of experience of differing contexts and perspectives.

Mentors are a great way of shortening your learning curve and building on the experience and perspectives of others. The best mentors make you think, freely share their experience and wisdom, and are prepared to open their networks to you. Never forget that these connections and contacts are the result of investment by your mentor. They are giving you something hard-earned and valuable. As such it needs to be treated with respect and courtesy.

Mentoring is an important way of developing your skills and understanding as a leader – especially when leading smart people. The insights of what worked and what did not, gleaned from others' experience or different perspectives, can save you time and money, and from making mistakes.

Example

Suki was an ambitious young architect, hard-working (perhaps too hard-working) and keen to make a success of her chosen profession. Although she had an excellent academic record, she knew that she needed help to navigate her way around the firm where she worked and make the progress she wanted. But how? She realised that there were a lot of things she needed to know and understand. A more senior colleague suggested that finding a mentor might be the best way to access the help she needed.

Suki regularly attended networking events and at one she met David, head of production for a local engineering firm. In their conversation, Suki found David had views and a perspective on leadership challenges that were different from her own. He was flattered when she asked him to act as a mentor. Over time they discussed a variety of issues. Their conversations were frank, open and always seemed to provide Suki with a renewed sense of purpose and confidence. David offered an important external viewpoint that always gave Suki a different perspective. True, he did not make decisions for her, nor did she blindly follow his advice. His input was clear and helpful and the basis for a discussion rather than anything more prescriptive. It covered things like the pluses and minuses of various projects, how to handle some tricky staffing issues, and how to get ready for career advancement.

He was not afraid to disagree with Suki and, most of all, genuinely cared. In time, she also found opportunities to repay David for his wise counsel: the mentoring became 'reversed' and she started to navigate David through the world of social media. When he stepped down from his firm, she helped him set up on LinkedIn, craft his social media profile, and deploy the technology he needed to make his new life as a consultant more productive.

Do this

→ **You need to drive it**
Your mentors are likely to be busy people too. Whilst they are likely to be flattered to be asked and will be willing to help you, they don't need another 'needy' person making demands on them. So you need to make it work, set the pace, set the agenda, be clear on what you are asking for and generally schedule to fit in with their requirements.

→ **Select your mentor(s) carefully**
The role of the mentor is to help you with your longer-term career ambitions. So your mentor needs to have had some career success. In addition to technical capability, long-term career success means navigating the politics and influence networks in the organisation. Your mentors should have a track record of doing so. Be clear on why you are asking each individual: they may ask you why they have been chosen.

→ **Think carefully about your purpose**
What do you need help with? This is an important question as it helps clarify who might

be a good mentor for you. It may be someone inside your firm or organisation. It might be someone outside. If it is new trends and technology, maybe a young person would be better: a 'reverse' mentor. It could be someone from a different background, upbringing or community to help your understanding of diversity. Don't just slip into seeking a stereotypical 'older' mentor. Other options may be more helpful for you.

→ **Don't confuse being mentored with sponsorship**
Be clear on the role(s) your mentors are playing in your career. Mentors help you grow and develop. Sponsors take an active role in helping you move onwards and upwards through the organisation. Some groups, such as minorities, find themselves over-mentored and under-sponsored – which means that their career progression may not be as fast and direct as they are expecting.

Always ask yourself: will this work for me in my environment? Your mentors will be delighted to help you, but they are not you, nor are they immersed in the day-to-day issues with which you are dealing.

→ Be critical, question and challenge, evaluate the advice

Listen carefully to what your mentors are saying and discuss whether what they did, or recommend, will work for you. If you don't think it will, let them know why and talk it through. It should be a discussion which helps to shape your views and actions going forward. Your mentor's advice is based on their best, but partial, understanding of the situation. They are relying on what you have told them in order to offer advice. If it does not quite fit, or seems to raise other issues, you need to challenge them. Your mentor may have become successful by debating the issues, and they may expect you to actively challenge their advice rather than passively implement it.

→ Think broadly

Often we seek mentors from our own industry or profession. And whilst it is true that professional firms and their like are different and more difficult to manage and lead, it can sometimes be really helpful to have a mentor from outside your own organisation. They can bring clarity and ask the questions that place your issues in a new light.

→ Agree 'ground rules'

Clearly this is not a formal written contract. It is rather an idea of how you would like to see the relationship work. What do you want to get from it? What do you want your mentor to do? How often to meet? Where? Successful mentoring relationships invariably have some ground rules; boundaries are important in making relationships work.

→ Periodically review the relationship

Ask yourself, are we *both* still getting value from this relationship. Is it time to call a halt, separate and add another mentor? If you or they or both of you think a change is right, then in your discussion be sure to ask if there is anyone that your current mentor would recommend or can introduce you to. And if you are parting, be sure to thank your mentor for all their help and to offer to help them in any way you can in the future.

→ **Become a mentor yourself**
Learn how to be a mentor yourself. Make yourself available to others. Maybe enrol in one of the many programmes where business people are mentoring students in college or just starting work. And change the focus of the advice above so that it applies to *you* as a mentor.

And remember

No matter what the stage of your career, you should have a mentor – maybe more than one. The big mistake most people make is to think that they should somehow come to resemble or be like their mentor, which raises issues about identity and authenticity. How do I stay true to oneself if I am being like a mentor? A better way is to view each of your mentors as having distinct sets of skills, capabilities and knowledge. Choose those skills, capabilities and the knowledge that you need to bridge gaps and incorporate into your routines. Under no circumstances try to become a clone.

Having a mentor is a great way of learning and getting insights from other more experienced leaders. Like all learning it needs to be built into your way of operating. It needs to be adapted so that it sits easily with you and becomes a natural part of your way of operating. Who will you ask to be your mentor(s)?

Networking

Smart leaders know that their personal and professional contacts are an asset, a really valuable resource, and that the ability to make those connections is an important competence to be developed. These things are not just nice to have. They are essential tools to enable the implementation of the leader's agenda for the business. And both the internal and external networks need investment.

Smart leaders are proactive about building relationships for both the short and the long term. They create a web of personal contacts and acquaintances to provide the support, feedback and resources needed to get things done. It makes them stand out and makes people seek them out, both inside and outside their own business.

However, many leaders, whilst they know that building and maintaining their networks is important work, do not give it the ongoing attention it really needs. It is also work that some feel they are not good at, or may ignore because of the pressures of everyday work. Building and maintaining an effective network is important and needs to be treated in a serious manner like any other business-critical task. Smart leaders ignore this at their peril.

Example

Kaito, a young associate, had just received his first box of business cards – just in time for a forthcoming business networking event he had been selected to attend. Kaito had grown up being told that you should not boast about yourself and to be modest about your achievements. How was he going to deal with this event? He decided to contact and observe the best business developer in his firm, Adrienne, who would also be attending.

Adrienne sent Kaito off to get the list of attendees and together they identified a selection of people whom they would approach and speak with. She explained the importance of researching each individual: their company, what was going on commercially in that company, their firm's experience and relationship with each company. Next, who were these people they were intending to meet? They pored over LinkedIn profiles and the firm's customer-relationship management data to try and get a 'feel' for them as people. Finally, for each person, they identified some key questions, issues or talking points that they could use at the event.

The day of the event came and went; it was tiring but a success. Adrienne had tutored Kaito well and as they debriefed – reading the scribbled notes in their notebooks and on the back of the business cards they had collected – they planned the immediate follow-up actions: an article to be sent, a connection to be made to someone else, and a phone call to another. Adrienne stressed the importance of timely follow-up which was rewarded with an invitation to a meeting for a further discussion about a topic they had started at the event. Kaito had been lucky. By tapping into the expertise of a more experienced and natural networker like Adrienne, he had learnt some basic networking skills that would serve him well as his career developed.

Do this

At events

→ **Do your preparation**
Research the event, who will be attending, and select a small group of people whom you wish to meet. Be clear in your mind why you want to meet those people and find out about them, their roles and their organisations.

→ **Initial impressions**
Make yourself stand out from the crowd. Have something in your introduction that makes you sound interesting, different. Practise your introduction and opening comments so that they flow naturally. First impressions count hugely.

→ **Make yourself memorable**
You have about 15 seconds to do this, so keep it to two sentences – clear, without jargon or abbreviations, concise. Be personable, engaging and friendly, and say something interesting.

→ **Perfect your 'pitch' or your 'brand'**
Prepare, recite and practise what you want to be your core message for a spontaneous situation. Then be creative about customising it to a prospect's needs so that they have a reason to contact you again.

→ **Always carry your business cards/contact details**
Keep them in accessible places in your bag, inside pocket, wallet or purse. Keep them fresh and ready to exchange at the right moment. When given a card, spend a few moments looking at it and asking a question around it – for example, the job title and what it entails. This is the person's identity and status in your hand so don't play with it or just place it into your pocket.

→ **Make it easy**
Have a number of topics in mind that you can use to initiate conversations. Most people don't relish the idea of going into a room full of strangers with a view to making conversation. So make it easy for them to join a conversation with you, which is much easier if you have a pre-prepared topic.

→ Keep a filing system

Insert the card details into your contacts database. Note where you met them and when, with any particular interests, professional or personal, that they shared. Do research to see if you or others know anyone in the same organisation.

→ Post-event – follow up immediately

Find a reason to follow up with the key people with whom you have spoken. If there is an outcome from your discussion – a phone call, email, sharing an article or setting a date to meet – then do it by the agreed time. It demonstrates professionalism and they will feel respected. It makes a contribution to the building of trust between you.

In general terms

→ Invest in your internal network

Build your network internally as well as externally, and at different levels in your organisation. Include superiors (decision-makers and key influencers), peers (allies and sounding boards) and subordinates (significant for delivery team members). Colleagues at all three levels are potential advocates for you as well as resources to help execute your agenda.

→ Practise reciprocity and diversity

Recommend and connect people to one another. This is part of how leaders of smart people get things done. Whether the connection is to a financial adviser or a plumber doesn't really matter: both have value. Above all resist the temptation to 'keep score'; just keep connecting with people – it always pays off in the long term.

→ Create and maintain the right network

Review and reflect the building of your network and what you will need at different stages of your career. Ask yourself: What is the purpose of my network? Where will I meet the right people? What will be my strategy and action to make sure it is always fit for purpose?

And remember

Think of your network as not just for you but as something that also helps others. With whom can you connect so as to help them at a personal, strategic or operational level?

Fostering a wide range of relationships of varying depth amongst a wide range of people – both in and out of your sector – builds your reputation and reach. It is like a team that you carry with you, a platform to enable execution and also to give you support. Smart leaders build their networks knowing that reciprocity ultimately pays off in the long run. And when they are responsible for networking events they make sure that the timings, venues and format enable them to achieve the maximum mix of people possible for their aims.

Our final point is that you should focus on building relationships, not business-card collections, and don't play the 'numbers game' on LinkedIn or other social media apps. It is not only the number of contacts you have but also how well you keep connected to them that matters. Your network reflects your brand which is more than your job title. It is also your reputation and reach and it requires sustained management.

Innovation and creativity

Market changes are making ever-more strenuous demands on organisations and people. The pressure to achieve advantage while at the same time dealing with ever-increasing demands from clients and customers, themselves being buffeted by new and differing commercial pressures, is plainly visible. The response to this pressure of simply doing more of what we did yesterday – but faster – was never a great solution. Today it makes even less sense. New thinking, new ideas and ways of working that connect the brainpower of smart people with the latest technology are the way forward.

Truly innovative/creative breakthroughs are rare things. Innovation often comes from marrying ideas from two or more different places to form or enable something new, or from *incremental* changes to products, services or processes. It's the curiosity that asks 'What would happen if we …?' and 'Why is this done like that there – how might we do that?'

But to enable and, more importantly, embed innovative mindsets and environments is not easy. It requires leaders to be able to tolerate, and accept, a degree of inefficiency, error, uncertainty and failure – often in a work environment that has a low tolerance for failure and error. Leading smart people means making sure you have fostered a culture where people feel safe enough to take risks and make the changes that are needed.

Example

Helmut was the chief people officer for a multinational company with ambitious growth plans. The nature of the business meant that growth would require an increase in head count of around 35 to 40 per cent. With this realisation came not only the interesting question of how to find a huge number of new people but also the more practical challenge of where they would be located. Helmut stopped and reflected, as the implications for their property requirement fully sank in. 'Do we really need 35 to 40 per cent more office space?', he wondered. Maybe there were other solutions he should consider.

The outcome from this one question was profound. It led in the first instance to a series of facilitated brainstorms with existing staff which triggered a raft of projects and innovative ideas – Helmut wanted nothing to be off limits at this stage. These initial ideas were then prioritised and analysed by smaller groups who investigated their feasibility in more detail. Case studies from other organisations and advisers were taken into account.

This was a lengthy and complex process which often threatened to generate more heat than light. But Helmut kept going and, in the end, the entire company had taken a serious relook at their office-space requirements. Flexible and remote working proved popular with people for all sorts of reasons, but were just the tip of the iceberg. The project looked at infrastructure much more widely, initiating the use of shared service centres and reviews of the processes by which the work was actually carried out, eventually leading to new working processes utilising artificial intelligence and machine learning.

Although none of the initiatives was completely new, their unique combination was groundbreaking in the sector. As the cost savings started to filter through, it became clear that this new approach was being emulated by other players.

Do this

→ **Horizon-scan**
Ask your clients what trends they are following and worried about; what impact is it having on them? Then apply them to your business. How might these things affect you, or provide insights or opportunities? Read widely and look for parallels in other industries. Attend conferences or academic symposia. What is going on out there? Are you seeing/hearing of repeat issues/patterns in different industries? What might these mean for you, your organisation and your clients?

→ **Reverse mentor**
Ask for one or more of your juniors to act as a reverse mentor – especially when it is something they know more about than you – don't be afraid to ask!

Get them to explain and help you get to grips with the latest ideas and trends, especially in media and technology.

→ **Ask why – lots – to get to the core purpose**
Try asking 'Why?' at least five times, when it is sensible and gives useful knowledge, not just because you can. Ask 'Why is that like that?', 'Why are we doing this?', 'Why are we paying for this?' That almost always brings you back to the root cause of why things are done as they are, and sometimes with surprising results. The original reason may no longer apply and things may be ready for innovation and change.

→ **Don't view innovation as a threat**
Innovation always brings opportunity. Explain why changes are necessary and provide a realistic assessment of the positives that will accrue. Smart humans will be able to create hundreds of reasons to justify the status quo and not making the change. We spend our lives building routines to make life easier and to reduce our cognitive load. New ways of doing things mean breaking existing patterns and ways of working.

→ **Retain your curiosity**
Set your curiosity free and try seeing things through others' eyes. Question the reason why things are as they are. How

would your children understand or explain the issues with which you are grappling? Children's explanations and ideas are invariably enlightening. Once a month read a new journal or newsfeed, or go and see or do something that is out of your comfort zone. What insight and ideas does it provide?

→ Make your team meetings innovative

Use team meetings or awaydays to invite guest speakers who are different or out of the ordinary. Try contrarian thinkers. A religious leader, someone from a not-for-profit or law enforcement. How and why do they do the things they do? What can you learn? The trick here is to get a different perspective, but then only to use it if it works in your context too.

→ Let people mess up

Let your people know that the occasional failure is OK. This is not a mandate for unilateral poor performance. Smart people need to know that if they have made every effort to do what they have been asked, and for good reasons things have not worked out, they will not be punished or penalised for trying something new. Remember that R&D (Research

and Development) spend does not always create positive outcomes, but it does provide learning and insight from the failures.

→ Reward those who have tried to do things differently

Make a point of sharing and praising good efforts. Highlight the work that went into the effort. Make sure what has been learnt is made very clear and shared. Consider instituting an award or reward for the effort involved in the innovation process, not just for the end results. But do make it clear that repeating the same mistake is not acceptable, and not learning from others' prior efforts is completely unacceptable.

→ Start small

Create an environment where measured trials are the norm. Run pilots, trial programmes or projects and small-scale efforts. Smart people like to see quick progress and can become impatient. They also like to be sure that they are not being set up to fail. It may be necessary to ensure people really understand that a main purpose is to learn. Ensure successes are shared and more importantly so is the learning.

→ **Take your team to new places**

Try going to new, different places for your awaydays or the occasional meetings and do take time to make the most of the location. Does it spark new ideas or are there parallels and insights that have been prompted by the unfamiliar surroundings?

→ **Make doing things differently part of your mission**

Expect people to bring new ideas and suggestions to team meetings and gatherings. Make space to discuss new ways of doing things at team meetings and in appraisal/performance reviews. Smart people detect lip service and will know if you are serious about their ideas and suggestions: your actions must match your words.

→ **Watch your language**

Think 'yes and' rather than 'yes but'. Ask for something rather than anything. Our choice of words has an important impact on how people comprehend what is being asked of them and how they construct their response. The word 'but' implies a blockage or negative – 'anything' is unfocused. 'Something' implies they have something to add.

And remember

Leading smart people means being brave enough to make decisions to enable them to do things better. The good news is that smart people, given the right climate, will share plenty of ideas and suggestions, learn quickly, and can and will adapt to new ways of working. The important point is to make sure that they are fully involved in the process of creating the new ways of working.

Remember, the skills and tools to innovate successfully do exist, but may not be part of the everyday work and skills for your people. Consider proven methodologies such as brainstorming, design thinking and creativity. If you do not have the specific expertise to facilitate this process, it may make sense to pay for outside help. But beware the fads and trends that promise 'How to brainstorm your way to success in five minutes a day'. Innovation is serious, hard work and if you are using 'bought-in' methodologies, make sure you fully involve your own smart people fully.

Managing stakeholders

Every leader has individuals or groups who have an interest in what they are doing at work. Some of these parties are more interested or influential than others and some more or less affected than others. These are your stakeholders. You are not alone. Everyone from your boss, your boss's boss, your team, your colleagues' teams, and especially everyone who might be impacted by the work you are doing – including clients and customers – counts as stakeholders.

The management of stakeholders is of vital importance to every leader. Because of the fluid nature of most organisations that employ smart people, the power structures that influence what gets done are driven by stakeholder influence. And with the ubiquity of today's technology, any affected party has the potential to express their views from anywhere in the world at any time. It can be either good news or bad news. So the question becomes: how to best manage your stakeholders?

Example

Xavier, a new business development lead, had been recruited to win more business and increase sales from a huge multinational corporation called Beladon Inc. that currently paid multimillion-dollar fees to a competitor of Xavier's company.

Over six months Xavier approached his task in three ways. First, he investigated what was known about Beladon Inc.: its current and likely future strategy. The team delved into Beladon's competitive environment and really got to understand the issues with which they were dealing. This provided insight into where they might be able to add value. Secondly, Xavier investigated the service offerings his new company could provide. With the team he matched them up with what they thought Beladon Inc. might need. He then networked within his own company to identify key stakeholders: those who knew about Beladon Inc., those who had sector knowledge, product knowledge and influence, either directly in the firm or with the prospective client. Xavier invited this wide range of knowledgeable people to join the nascent client service team in whatever capacity they could, in order to help with the sales effort for Beladon Inc.

Thirdly, and concurrently, Xavier worked at developing contacts in Beladon Inc. itself. He found the key influencers and decision-makers: the important stakeholders. Xavier prepared a detailed 'stakeholder map', identifying business areas by geography and key individuals. At the subsequent team offsite meeting this stakeholder map was further developed by agreeing 'best-fit' colleagues. Their role was to meet and 'person-mark' and communicate with their opposite numbers in Beladon Inc. Xavier invited his colleagues to propose others they thought should be invited to join the team.

This process of actively managing the stakeholders involved, both internal and external, was widely credited as a key activity in increasing the revenues earned from Beladon Inc. to £30 million from a very small base of less than £1 million.

Do this

→ **Consider your stakeholders**
Think widely about the people who are involved in, or impacted by, your agenda. Who might 'win' or be advantaged? Who might 'lose'? These are stakeholders you need to consider. Make a list of their names. Some will have formal power and authority over your projects and interests and can actively help or hinder you. Others, without formal authority, may still be able to exert influence – again to help or hinder.

→ **Position your stakeholders in a 2 x 2 stakeholder map**
Plot them by name on the following matrix according to their influence on you (and others connected to your agenda), and their power to impact on what you are trying to achieve.

High

Authority

Low

Low   Influence   High

Use a different strategy for each quadrant of the matrix to manage your communication and relationship. Once categorised into a quadrant of the matrix, adopt an appropriate strategy to manage your relationships.

→ **Establish a communication strategy for each group in your matrix**
Update those with power/authority and influence constantly: keep them close and keep them engaged. Those with power/authority but less influence also need to be kept close, for example, by regular and careful management. Those with little power and influence still need monitoring and occasional updates. You never know when their status might change.

→ **Always deliver your communications on time and regularly**
Agree a flow and detail for your communication with stakeholders. Equally important is making sure your communications always arrive at the 'right' time. This

requires an understanding of your stakeholders' needs to judge when your communication update will be best received. Be sure to provide the information in a format that is easy for your stakeholders to digest and use for their purposes. If you are delivering a bulletin later than originally agreed, make sure that you manage expectations.

→ Look for connections between stakeholders

Find out who has worked together in the past, because past work allegiances carry forward. Be prepared to look a long way back. Look for non-obvious connections. Assuming the connections are real, you might have another source of information or influence that explains stakeholder behaviour.

→ Build and reinforce your stakeholder base

Be clear with your stakeholders about how you would like them to help and why you are asking them. And have good motives – seek out those who might aid your agenda or endeavours for the 'right' reasons. They will understand that you are trying to implement projects and make changes in an ambiguous environment. Successful implementation needs the involvement of the influence networks in the organisation. When you are dealing with smart people they 'get it' and will understand why you have approached them.

→ Don't see things that are not there

Treat all information with care and caution. But don't over- or underestimate the importance of a shared university, club or association membership. In the real world, coincidence does happen, but connections may be in our own minds and have no bearing on how people behave in the here and now.

→ Constantly maintain your radar

Be vigilant: the way power shifts in knowledge-based organisations is unpredictable. When someone is promoted, moved, joins or leaves it has potential impact elsewhere on your influence network. You need to keep track of who is moving into and out of influence in your universe. More worrying are the influencers who appear out of 'left field'; plan so that you are not taken by surprise.

→ Be sensitive

Think about how you work within the organisational hierarchy. For example, your boss's boss is a stakeholder in your efforts. This implies a 'chain of command' that should be followed. Consider how your boss will feel if you have gone over his or her head to instigate a discussion without their knowledge and approval.

→ **Reach out**

Make time to reach out and communicate on a one-to-one basis with your stakeholders, ideally in person and across your entire stakeholder group. You do not need an excuse. Simply telling people in person that you want to keep in touch is good. Even better is asking for their advice and help. People rarely refuse requests for help. But do act on the advice; smart people hate feeling that they have wasted their precious time.

And remember

Stakeholder management has never been more important and is a key part of the strategy to successfully deliver your objectives in any organisation. Not recognising new 'players' when they arrive on the scene, or a change in the power or influence in existing players, can have a huge impact on your ability to deliver. This is not a once-only activity, though; it needs constant monitoring. The fluid nature of modern organisations means that power, influence and alliances are constantly on the move. As a minimum, revisit and update your stakeholder map regularly. Similarly, even though you may know these people, don't assume they are up to date with the goings-on in your world: you will have to be explicit with your requests to most of them.

Storytelling

One of the most powerful tools any smart leader has is their ability to communicate messages, ideas and possibilities. As humans we have developed sophisticated ways of transmitting these things to other humans, and one of the most impactful is still through the telling of stories.

For the leader of smart people, your credibility is in part based on your experience and your ability to reference that experience in a subtle and modest way that is coherent and memorable for the current and next generations of leaders. Since time immemorial, humans have passed on wisdom through stories, at first round campfires, now around coffee machines and water coolers (the linking factor being food and drink).

For smart people, who absorb facts, concepts and theory pretty quickly, stories have the benefit of providing the all-important context that makes the lessons valuable and immediately applicable. So for the leader of smart people, stories, based on your experiences of what has gone well and where you have struggled, are essential ways of transmitting learning and meaning and values. They are authentic and real. But do make sure you draw out the relevant points you want your people to remember.

Example

A tale of two leaders

Stefan was smart, bright, charismatic and elected to lead his firm in the footsteps of an equally larger-than-life leader. He was permanently on the move – a veritable action man – so busy, rushing from meeting to meeting, that he was occasionally very poorly prepared. One morning, he made his usual hasty arrival for a meeting with senior colleagues. He concluded his address with one of his 'stock' stories. Unfortunately, all of the assembled company had heard the story many times before. His story landed poorly and reinforced the fact that he was rushed and had not prepared. His credibility took a hard blow and that meeting was generally believed to be the beginning of the end of his tenure. The impact of that one story was often cited as a key turning point.

Philip was a thoughtful and understated leader, at least in behavioural terms. A voracious reader, he had assembled an array of stories and added to them regularly. Some were his own stories, others ones that he had accumulated from his reading and adapted. To add to his store of stories, he also developed a style of delivery that made people want to listen. His people were always amazed that he seemed to have stories ready to illustrate important issues. More importantly, his stories were fresh and relevant and always fit for the occasion and the audience concerned. Philip was promoted regularly and became recognised as one of the most influential leaders in his organisation.

Do this

→ **Build a fund of stories**
Think back through your career. What have been the seminal experiences that have taught you lessons? Note them down in a book, journal or computer file. And read and use others' stories – but always acknowledge the provenance.

→ **Remember that powerful stories don't just happen**
Construct powerful stories that you can trial and refine. Each of your stories needs crafting. You need to have characters to whom people can relate. Powerful stories have an emotional 'hook', something that makes the listener care about the people involved, a challenge or dilemma to make the listener think and remember. They also have a resolution so as to bring closure.

→ **Remember the structure of a good story**
Structure your stories with a beginning, a middle and an end. Have a restatement of the key message at the end. A good story introduces characters and helps us understand them and form a judgement about them.

It makes us think. It makes us remember. Remember and use the structure of children's nursery rhymes.

→ **Make sure you have a people element**
Construct your stories so that people can connect to the people in your story emotionally. It is the feeling of being in another's shoes and the dilemmas/challenges and drama of human existence that people remember. Most importantly, make sure the listener will empathise with the characters.

→ **'Paint' pictures**
Use your words and language to construct a graphic, rich context against which your stories play out. Help your listeners 'see' the story unfold. Give them clues and background to make a rich panorama. As the story progresses, help them to connect with it at a visual as well as simply auditory level. The richer the context and clues, the more real it becomes and that will improve the emotional impact too.

→ Be human

Make sure some of your stories reflect your own trials, challenges and failures. Your people are smart. Treating them to a diet of nothing but successes will be a huge turn-off. They know you have messed up at times. So, sharing your failings and what and how you have learnt from those occasions makes you more accessible as a leader, and more human. More importantly it makes people want to follow you as you seem to be more like them.

→ Be clear on the 'moral' or lesson of your story

Make sure you are clear at the end of your story about the point you are using your story to illustrate. You can only be responsible for the transmission of your story, not what others take from it. Don't patronise your audience, but make sure your conclusion is crystal-clear.

→ Study other storytellers

Read and study the classics: Aesop, Hemingway, Dickens, Sun Tzu. Kierkegaard, Kipling, Hesse. The great storytellers of days gone by knew how to connect people and their storytelling has stood the test of time. Read (or reread) a selection to remind yourself what really good storytelling looks like. And to come bang up to date, most TED talks are well scripted, structured and delivered – watch and learn.

→ Reach a wide audience

Use technology to help spread your message. One way of spreading your message that helps reinforce your leadership reputation is to make sure you reach a wider audience. Fortunately technology has the answer – so use it to your advantage. Start blogging, or use LinkedIn or your company's internal mechanisms.

→ Keep it fresh

Refresh your story stock regularly. Being a master storyteller means having something new to say. That means constantly building and refining your fund of stories. There is nothing worse than repeating a favourite tale at every opportunity and not realising how inappropriate it may be at some of those opportunities. Smart people will feel patronised and taken for granted. Moreover, it conveys the message that you have not prepared and that your audience is not important.

And remember

Being a great leader means building upon your experiences –
the good and the bad. It also means being able to share those
experiences in a compelling way. Stories enhance your technical
knowledge and experience. So use your experience as the basis
for a variety of authentic impactful stories, a ready supply based
on your own experience.

Smart people don't just need textbook answers. They can
read textbooks themselves. They want the subtleties and the
nuances. They want to hear from people they respect, who have
lived a little, and most importantly who are generous enough to
share the mistakes from which they have learnt. One proviso:
your stories should not have too much embellishment. Smart
people have a finely honed ability to sniff out inconsistencies and
detect over-exaggeration.

Strategy

A strategy is the way in which a firm or practice intends to achieve sustainable competitive advantage over time. No business competes in a vacuum, so there will always be competitors who will try to frustrate your efforts. Part of your strategy will be to consider how you deal with them.

To be clear, a strategy is not an objective or destination. A strategy is the manner you choose to reach that destination. It is worth bearing in mind this distinction as you start to think about your organisation's destination. All too often, strategies become overcomplicated. Great ones have an elegance that allows them to be easily communicated. Your strategy, once agreed, will need to be communicated numerous times, so constructing a simple (but not simplistic) narrative is key. A good strategy is only deliverable if it involves others, and it needs to impact on the day-to-day work of the people in the organisation, so engagement and consultation are essential.

Example

Fernando had been watching the trends in his marketplace for many months. And the more he observed, the more he came to realise that his group needed to change direction. He gathered intelligence and spoke often and at length about this with his partners. Gradually they formed a collective view of the marketplace and which customers and clients they should be serving to make optimal use of the skills, talents and resources in their group.

Fernando instigated conversation with his colleagues about which sectors of the market they should attack; which clients and customers they should be serving with what products and services; and which clients and customers they should disengage from. They discussed how they might make changes to the way they staffed jobs and used technology, how they would price the work, and how all of the changes aligned with the entire firm's strategy. Crucially they had detailed conversations about how their competitors were likely to react and how Fernando's team should respond.

All of the above resulted in a revised business plan with detailed actions; who would be doing what, by when and with whom. While this entire process was not quick, it was as fast as Fernando could make it – consistent with making sure everyone had their say. It was also based on rigorous analysis, clearly messaged, and above all agreed by the extended leadership coalition. This enabled the entire team to move into action very quickly afterwards and take the necessary steps towards the agreed goals.

Do this

→ **Realise that a strategy is actually three pieces of work**
Your main overt task is to set a direction for the department or practice group. Task number two is to use the leadership opportunity to build engagement with the team. The third task is ensuring that your teams have the capability and resources to deliver. You need to weave these three elements together skilfully.

→ **Set the direction of travel**
Clarity over direction of travel is paramount – and difficult. The leader needs to select a direction of travel that is stretching and challenging for the team members, both personally and technically. It does not have to be so far 'out there' that it is discouraging, nor so easy that the team wonder why they are bothering. The smart leader selects a direction, aligned with the organisation's objectives, and then 'sense-tests' it with their leader and some trusted confidant(e)s. Leaders of smart people typically struggle with setting direction, often because they do not feel they have the right to so do, or are worried about the reaction. Getting it right is critical if you want to achieve anything.

→ **Get others on board – build engagement with the team**
Smart people don't like being told what to do; they need to feel invested and involved in the process of determining where they are going. So how do you get them to do what you want them to do? By constantly articulating and socialising the ideas. Don't deliver faits accomplis unless you have said that is what you will do. And beware of the likely fallout from those who disagree with you and decide to take their 'smarts' elsewhere.

→ **Use the leadership opportunity**
What style will you adopt? How will others feel that they are being treated? Smart people are usually very marketable. So keeping them on board and feeling committed is the task for the leader. This is helped by a continuous series of conversations and taking appropriate decisions at appropriate times.

→ **Agree your desired result with your 'boss' and link it directly to the firm's direction and objectives**

Have the necessary conversations and test that the desired end point is what is needed and aligned to the objectives of the wider organisation. Check this out with your peer leaders. Ask for their opinions and ideas. See where you can help them – and they you.

→ **Get buy-in/commitment to the end goal before you start**

Do *not* present your ideas as fully formed and a game plan for your colleagues to execute. Smart people resent diktats and instructions; as a minimum they will implement reluctantly. You need input from your colleagues for two reasons: (a) to get a more thought-through solution and (b), more importantly, to ensure that they are committed to executing the solution. Ask for their ideas and make sure you use them or at least acknowledge them.

→ **Build a team – you can't do it on your own!**

Life with smart people is invariably a team game. Team games need all the players to know which game they are playing and what rules they are playing to. Having a team around you extends your influence more widely in the firm. It also makes it easier to implement ideas.

→ **Communicate like never before, and make sure others do too**

Use every opportunity to reinforce and share your messages. In times of change, you need to communicate honestly and regularly: the successes, the failures, wins, losses, progress and setbacks. Make sure your communication is balanced with the good and the not-so-good. Your colleagues are smart, capable people; treat them as such.

→ **Consider who might try and hinder you, why and how they might do so**

Implementing a strategy – especially in a professional environment – is an inherently political activity. (See the section on Politics and influence, p. 186.) Listen more than you talk, and listen to people across the business. If feedback indicates that you need to act, then do so, but make sure you involve others in your activity.

→ **Keep your air cover intact**
Make sure your supporters are onside and so is your boss. Keep both groups constantly in the picture and crucially ask them for *their* views on progress and on what you are doing. What are they hearing out in the business or wider world? Ask for their advice and counsel; what do they think your next steps should be?

And remember

There is a real tendency for smart people to overcomplicate things. It is something we have often seen in groups of bright, sharp, able people. So 'keep it simple and do it to death'. Resist the siren call of your colleagues who are looking for something bright, shiny and new because results have not materialised in two weeks. Perseverance and discipline are essential. Manage expectations. This is not to advocate blind adherence to the strategy for all time. Clearly there are times when change is warranted and necessary. Our experience says that changes to strategy are often made too early and too often, usually before the strategy has had a fighting chance of delivering the desired results.

Equally, there is often a demand for 'the answers' and a prescription: 'Tell us what to do.' This too should be avoided, as engagement amongst smart people is a key element of gaining their willing commitment. Smart people need to make sense of the strategy themselves, they need to get involved and start trying to contribute themselves.

Vision

If you are going to lead, you need to have a starting idea for a destination. After all if you don't know where you are wanting to go, why should others follow you? Your team members will certainly expect you to have an idea, but they also expect to have a meaningful say in that future and the opportunity to craft what that destination will look like. Moreover you need their best ideas to put with your own, to create a compelling, uplifting vision that positions the firm for future success.

There is no point in being a leader with a vision that people don't follow. Smart people need to have a say in the destination *and* the proposed mode of travel. Leaders who ignore this need for involvement do so at their peril. This means understanding the meaning behind what is being proposed and squaring it away in their own minds as something they can believe in and, as a minimum, can be useful and worthy of their efforts and investment. Inviting the team to shape the vision and subsequent strategy and tactics for achieving it is an essential part of bonding the team with you and each other and the wider organisation.

Example

Felice had recently been appointed managing partner from being practice group head for the CCEG (Construction and Civil Engineering Sector Group) in his law firm. He led the group that had built a great reputation in the market for its ability to manage legal relationships in complex property development projects. But the firm was being threatened by nimbler niche boutiques eyeing the rich pickings and entering 'their' market.

This worried Felice, but he had also come to a stunning realisation that CCEG had a hitherto hidden core competence. Helped by his mentor, he realised that a burgeoning area of law in large IT development projects mirrored legal relationships in CCEG. He tested his understanding to confirm his thinking and then set about formulating a new specialisation for the firm that included IT law. He actively invited questions and challenges from stakeholders throughout his organisation, and listened and probed until he was clear that his initial assumptions were correct.

Felice carefully communicated how this new venture could really make a big difference for the firm as a whole. His vision was built on the idea of taking the firm's technical legal capability to become their clients' number 1 choice for both CCEG and major IT projects. It was a sensible and achievable expansion that would build on and reinforce the firm's current market position.

Once his group was on board with the vision in principle, they worked together on a written vision statement that encapsulated neatly what they looked to achieve, a useful shorthand for both internal and external stakeholders who did not need the more detailed strategic and tactical programme the team successfully implemented to make their vision a reality.

Do this

→ **Bridge the current reality to the new vision**

Prepare the way, ensuring that others can follow by defining goals and showing how they are attainable. Smart people will make links between where they see themselves and where you, their leader, are proposing to take them. If they think it is completely unattainable they will not be convinced they should sign up.

→ **Create a shared vision**

Start with some initial *and incomplete* ideas and start to share them. Make it crystal-clear this is initial thinking and a collaborative effort to build something bigger and better than any individual can do on their own. The leader's responsibility is to get the best ideas and input from a lot of smart people and collectively craft them into something you can all rally behind to build a better future place.

→ **Make the vision live**

Take every opportunity to share the vision and initiate action and steps towards making it become a reality. The vision needs to become more than just words – it needs to become alive and visible for the people. The leader's role is to energetically remind and rally people behind the vision and the steps being taken to make it come alive.

→ **Paint a vivid, aspirational picture of the future for your organisation**

A vision states where an organisation is going. Make it long-term (18 to 24 months) and agree appropriate, stretching metrics with the team. Make it something that connects with people at an emotional level. To be understood, it needs to be crystal-clear about what the destination will look, feel and sound like. Getting the right blend of aspiration and challenge will be key.

→ **Set out the strategy for the route to achieve your vision**

Creating a vision means articulating a place of advantage for your business in your sector; it is about anticipating and planning for market changes. All these factors contribute to strategic thinking. Strategy cannot be formulated without knowing the destination. Vision provides this overarching goal; strategy the means to achieve it.

→ Build in short- and long-term goals

The strategic journey to the vision should have milestones against which the entire team can monitor progress. You need to be able to build in and celebrate short-term wins that will help achieve long-term goals.

→ Create a vision statement

A vision statement should be a clear, brief statement of intent. Write it in the present tense, make it emotive – instil passion. Summarise the vision statement into a short, pithy powerful phrase that is distinctive and impactful and that people can easily grasp and identify with. And ask your team to critique it before going public.

→ Clarity is key

Forget buzzwords and corporate-speak and ignore the temptation to use slogans or simplistic alliteration. Use language that is easily understood, unambiguous, and as simple as possible. And if you are going to use an acronym or a slogan, make sure that some witty individual cannot have fun with it by twisting the meaning or rephrasing it.

→ Ensure every person understands

Communicate and discuss the vision with everyone who will be charged with making it a reality. Remember: a vision statement drives not just what they will do, but also how they will go about doing it.

→ Keep it under review

Regularly review the statement and metrics. Are they still relevant? Have things changed? Is everyone still on course and doing what is needed? What does the team think? If things are changing, then a team conversation is needed about changes and revisions.

And remember

The art of creating a vision makes two demands on leaders. The first is to orchestrate and manage the human dynamics in the team so as to enable a vision to be created. The second is to cope with the uncertainty that comes from relinquishing control to allow others to be able to make a significant contribution to the destination and the journey. The role is to enable the team.

To be inspiring and uplifting your vision needs to be 'big picture' and go beyond the technical, numeric and issues of day-to-day management. It needs to engage, energise and enable local decision-making to drive productive action in the business. The vision has to be realistic and not so far 'out there' as to be unattainable. Above all it needs to have been built with the initiative, creativity and involvement of the team – it is their efforts and commitment that will determine how well it is executed.